MW00387911

JIMI HENDRIX:

Designed by Arnold Skolnick

A Chameleon Book

REFLECTIONS AND VISIONS

BY NONA HATAY

Pomegranate Artbooks, San Francisco, California

A CHAMELEON BOOK

Published by Pomegranate Artbooks
Box 6099
Rohnert Park, California 94927

Pomegranate Europe Ltd.
Fullbridge House, Fullbridge
Maldon, Essex CM9 7LE England

Produced by Chameleon Books
211 West 20th Street
New York, New York 10011

For information about *PhotoArtWorks:*
Collector's Special Editions
Box 182
Montague, Massachusetts 01351

Library of Congress Cataloging-in-Publication Data

Hatay, Nona.
Jimi Hendrix : reflections and visions / by Nona Hatay : designed by Arnold Skolnick.
p. cm.
ISBN 0-87654-480-4
1. Hendrix, Jimi—Pictorial works. 2. Rock Musicians—United States—Pictorial works. I. Title.
ML88.H44H37 1995
787.87 ' 166 ' 092—dc20
[B] 95-9597
CIP
MN

Designed by Arnold Skolnick
Editorial Assistant: Mary Serreze
Production Assistant: Nona Hatay

Printed by Oceanic Graphic Printing, Hong Kong
00 99 98 97 96 95 6 5 4 3 2 1

First Edition

This book has been produced with the approval of the Hendrix family and permission from Are You Experienced? Inc.

Madison Square Garden Review, p 16: *Variety* magazine, May 21, 1969.
Quote by Johnny Winter, p 80: *Hendrix—A Biography*, Chris Welsh (Omnibus Press, 1972).
Quote by John McLaughlin, p 113: *The Hendrix Portfolio*, Nona Hatay (Studio Hatay, 1978).
Quote by Bob Dylan, p 24: Unreleased CD (© 1988 Special Ryder Music), liner notes.
Quotes by Noel Redding, Mitch Mitchell, James Brown, and Taj Mahal: *Jimi Hendrix, the Spirit Lives On . . .* (© Hatay, published, Last Gasp, San Francisco, 1984).
Quotes by Billy Cox and Vernon Reid: St*one Free: A Tribute to Jimi Hendrix* Interview CD (Reprise Records).Produced by Katrina Fernandez.
Quote by Felix Pappalardi, p 87: *Superstars In Their Own Words*,interview by Sue C. Clark, ed. Douglas Kent (Music Sales USA, 1970).
Quotes by Hendrix, pp 17, 26, 35, 78, 97, 106, 108, 109: *Superstars In Their Own Words*,interview by Sue C. Clark, ed. Douglas Kent (Music Sales USA, 1970)
Quote by Hendrix, p 24: *Jimi Hendrix: In His Own Words*, Tony Brown (Music Sales USA, 1995).
Quote by Hendrix, p 95: Brochure, The Jimi Hendrix Foundation, 1995. Hendrix Lyrics: *Jimi Hendrix Songbook* (unpublished). Lyrics reprinted with permission from Are You Experienced? Inc. and Bella Godiva Music, Inc.
Hendrix Hand Writings, pp 37, 117, 128: *Cherokee Mist: The Lost Writings*, ed. Bill Nitopi (HarperCollins, 1994).

ACKNOWLEDGMENTS

I wish to offer special thanks to the following:

Gail Archibald, Jerome Preston Bates, Tony Beard, Chris Berger, Joan Boudin-Price, David Bourbeau, Rosa Lee Brooks, Tony Brown, Taylor Buczynski, Sue C. Clark, Kayla Cleveland, Ira Jay Cohen, Monika Dannemann, Alice de Young, Wini Dean, Guy DeVito, Kingsley Fairbridge, Andy Feiler, Richard Flanzer, Rita Fletcher, Steven Jay Gabe, Judy Gage, Peter Gezork, Caesar Glebbeek, Sherry Goodman, Kaitlin Harrison, Charles Hatay, Pamela Hatay-Stratton, Al Hendrix, Janie Hendrix, Bob & Big Al Jurkowski, Guru Nam Khalsa, David Kramer, Master D.K., John McDermott, John McLaughlin, Bill Myers, Network Chiropractors: Wayne Garfinkel, Jeffrey Goldwasser, and Dan Garfield, Bill Nitopi, Richard Opper, "Prez" Pieraccini, Phyz, James Propert, Tara Quinn, Steve Roby, Rickie Rouse, S.F. Photo Center, Tammy Schatz, Mary Serreze, Carl Sesar, Arnold Skolnick, Don Snyder, John Stahl, David Stratton, Mark Thayer, Ken Voss N.H.

DEDICATION
For my son, Charles Hatay-Gezork, my daughter Heidi Merris, and son-in-law Chris D'Arco; of course Jimi Hendrix and the Spirit of Love & Good & God in us all . . .

INTRODUCTION BY NONA HATAY
7

THE *PHOTOARTWORK* OF NONA HATAY BY SHERRY GOODMAN
9

JIMI HENDRIX 1942–1970 BY JYM FAHEY
13

THE CONCERT, MAY 18, 1969
16

1970s BLACK & WHITE EXPERIMENTS
20

THE HENDRIX PORTFOLIO
44

1980s COLOR EXPANSIONS
48

PARIS, FRANCE
99

LONDON, ENGLAND
101

1990s TECHNOART
103

REMEMBERING JIMI
118

THE SPIRIT LIVES ON
121

CONTRIBUTORS
122

PHOTOARTWORK TITLES
124

CHRONOLOGY AND EXHIBITION HISTORY
125

AFTERWORD BY ZENO ROTH
127

CONTRIBUTORS

Carlos W. Anderson
Jimy Bleu
Larry Blumenstein
Joel Brattin
Rosa Lee Brooks
James Brown
Sean Cinemaie
Ari Freeman Cohen
Ira Cohen
Julie Coryell
Billy Cox
Michael Caruso
Paul Caruso
Monika Dannemann
Jenni Dean
John Dubberstein
Max Drake
Jym Fahey
Michael "Bongo" Grabscheid
Sherry Goodman
Cornelius Grant
James Al Hendrix
James Hendrix Sundquist
Du Kane
Charlie Karp
Timothy Leary
Taj Mahal
Emmaretta Gloria Marks
Yazid Manou
Fred McDarrah
John McLaughlin
Mitch Mitchell
Felix Pappalardi
Lenee Jean Pierre
Kenny Pine
Noel Redding
Vernon Reid
Zeno Roth
Lars Skanberg
Emikan Sudan
Robin Sylvester
Ben Valkhoff
Norman Weisberg
Johnny Winter

As I believe Jimi Hendrix was more than just an important figure in pop history, more than just a great musician and entertainer, I feel it is important to finally put him in perspective—by taking into account not only the years he was active in a physical sense, but the whole period of our century. Jimi to me was a truly significant artist and messenger of this century, trying to fight egotism and materialism and to convey that only *together* mankind will be able to solve the problems it shares. I therefore believe that those who recognize Jimi's significance should put their energies together, aiding each other and trying to create a new approach to Jimi's message and mankind's destiny. So I truly hope that we can find a way of working together.

—Zeno Roth

INTRODUCTION

When I photographed Jimi Hendrix in 1969, little did I know what an extensive artistic project would evolve. From the negatives of that one concert at Madison Square Garden, I have produced over 500 one-of-a-kind experimental black & white photographs and hand- painted *PhotoArtWorks*. Most of them are directly inspired by a specific song. The creative challenge has been to bring the essence and spirit of Hendrix's music and lyrics into the still photograph.

Choosing the *PhotoArtWorks* for this book has given me the chance to review 25 years of my Hendrix art. I had to decide which pieces are important to include — not only to me personally but to the collection as a whole. I noticed that I have some favorite images that I go back to often, printing and painting in different ways, as well as some pictures that I've printed just once and there are even some shots of the concert I've never printed.

My work on Hendrix has gone through various phases. Over the years, I've experimented with different artistic and photographic styles and techniques, and have then put the negatives aside to work on other projects. At times, I've thought that I'd never create another Hendrix piece, only to be reinspired by Hendrix's music.

At first, this book was to portray just *PhotoArtWorks*, with minimal text by Hendrix. But part of my great Hendrix Experience has been meeting people who share my love and appreciation of Jimi Hendrix and his music. I decided to include a few of these people's comments. But the response was so abundant that soon I had too much written material—so I have been able to include only the "tip of the iceberg". The Spirit does live on!

I am grateful for this opportunity to blend visual art, words, and color to create a tribute to the great musician,composer, and writer, Jimi Hendrix. —Nona Hatay

Looking at Nona's art, I am reminded of the purpose of true art. . . not so much to be enjoyed but to illuminate. Here in the western world, art is seldom what it's meant to be—or what it has always been to the ancients—a means of invoking a consciousness of the realm beyond the senses. Her "art as magic" has a most compatible flow with Hendrix's "sound as magic" —Jimy Bleau

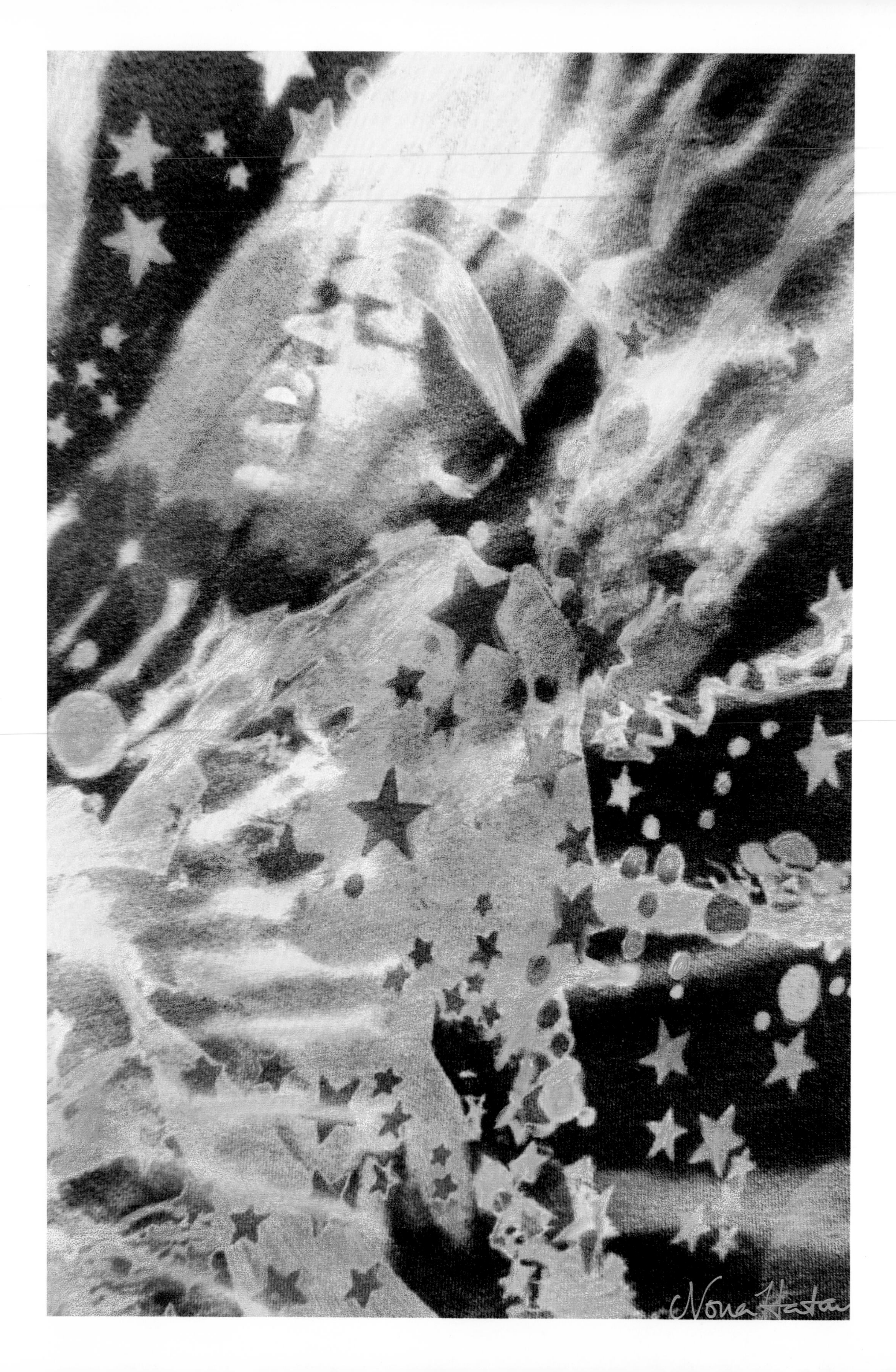

THE *PHOTOARTWORKS* OF NONA HATAY

IN NONA HATAY'S *ASTRO MAN*, a radiant aura of trailing stars accompanies Jimi Hendrix as he makes a cosmic appearance in space, on stage, in the mind's eye. "Before I remember anything," Hendrix once said, "I remember music and stars and planets." And Nona Hatay remembers Hendrix in her striking *PhotoArtWorks*, where time—documented, recalled, exploded—takes color and shape.

*Jimi Hendrix: Visions and Reflection*s unfolds a twenty-year vision of Hatay's artistic interpretations of Hendrix as musician and creative force. Beginning with the black & white negatives shot by Hatay—then a young freelance photojournalist—at Madison Square Garden in May of 1969, it chronicles the development of her career as an artist: first, her experiments with interpretive black & white printing, then her forays into hand-coloring and media-layering, and finally her more recent venture into the world of high-technology photo-imaging.

In Hatay's *PhotoArtWorks*, the experimental black-& white photographs are the fixed, first-and-forever impression, the structure. In 1975, while listening to *Voodoo Child* in her darkroom, Hatay began multi-printing the negatives, solarizing in the style of Man Ray, and playing with a number of unusual techniques, creating a series of innovative prints that stand on their own.

I Hear My Train

Color is a more recent dimension of Hatay's experimental photoart. She has hand-colored the black & white experimental prints intuitively, selectively, interpretively, as if reaching back in time to actually touch her experience of Hendrix in concert. When Hatay combines the mediums of paint and photography, a new multi-dimensional world occurs. In it, vision and touch, past and present, fixed and fluid, reality and surreality coexist.

Purple Haze

Visually, the black & white image surfaces through the overlay of color in her later works. The subtle intervention of color shifts mood or atmosphere, rendering each print unique. Sometimes color shades the entire image, as in the melancholy chill blue of an early version of *Purple Haze*. At other times, color singles out an element such as Hendrix's illuminated clothing in *I Hear My Train A Comin'*, where his black & white face, hands, and guitar are left stark and exposed.

This distinctive partial coloring produces elusive and mysterious effects in Hatay's images. When Hendrix ignites with color, glowing with magical presence on stage (*Jimi's Back*), his polychrome image separates inner and outer reality, music and everyday life. When Hendrix remains a spectral black & white figure sur-

Jimi's Back

Opposite: *Astro Man*

Wild Thing

rounded by color, the image suggests both presence and absence. Apart from symbolic references, partial coloring also parallels how we experience and recall reality itself. We register and remember aspects of our lives in light of their emotional "coloring"—memory paints the pictures of the mind selectively.

Hatay's hand-colored photographs are sometimes compared with pop-artist Andy Warhol's photography-derived silk-screens. Like Hatay, Warhol subjected images of media icons to endless color variations. But Warhol's images belong to the world of commercial printing. Their intentional off-register effects suggest a mechanical metamorphosis. Hatay, on the other hand, tends to free her color from the underlying shape, as seen dramatically in her wax crayon coloring *Wild Thing*, where color coexists loosely with shape and behaves like a force of free fantasy.

Postmodernism offers a broad and provocative context for appreciating Hatay's approach. Many postmodern artists use photography as their primary medium and juxtapose other media with it to achieve unexpected effects. David Salle, for example, layers cartoon-like, Day-Glo outline images transparently over black & white figures. Postmodernists often combine self-conscious visual quotations from both high and low art. Unlike Hatay, however, their work tends to be more intellectual, detached, and ironic than emotional and spiritual.

Hatay's use of color finds closer parallels in cinematography. A number of notable films have used black & white and color together to create emotional or temporal effects similar to Hatay's. In Spielberg's *Schindler's List,* even before the much remarked-upon color ending, there is a scene where a young girl makes her way unharmed through a crowd during a Nazi raid. Her brightly colored red dress amid the black & white footage poignantly traces her path for the viewer. In a different spirit is the classic *The Wizard of Oz*, where black & white sequences give way to color, reinforcing the transition between reality and fantasy in the story itself.

An interesting connection can be made between the inherent musicality of Hatay's photoart and the modernist search for evocative relationships among the different senses. During the dynamic era of early abstraction, artists saw color as a visual analogue to sound, and explored the idea that color can elicit an emotional response from the viewer akin to music's effect. The Russian artist Wassily Kandinsky, for example, experienced the color orange as "ringing out like a church bell." The heightened, unexpected, sometimes sharp colors in Hatay's photoart can be described as "electric"—a visual equivalent to the sounds of Hendrix's electric guitar.

In From the Storm

The musical quality of Hatay's photo art also arises from her experiments with form and composition. Note, for example, the rhythmic repetition of shape in a recent version of *Purple Haze* entitled *In From the Storm* where Hendrix's image echoes infinitely back into space. Visual syncopation, the suggestion of melodic line, dissonance, and harmonic resolution all find play in her formal constructions.

Many of Hatay's images possess mythic or archetypal overtones. Turning toward a dark passage down an unknown way, Hendrix's melancholy face in *Electric Lady Studios* suggests the Greek myth of the poet-singer Orpheus who is fated to return to the underworld in search of his love. In the complex and unsettling *Voodoo Child*, Hendrix assumes the form of a black cat—a suggestion of the artist's animus, or magical metamorphosis through music. The metaphysical allusions are not necessarily intentional; rather, they spring unguarded from the archetypal plane on which Hatay artistically experiences her subject.

Electric Lady Studios

Hatay achieves a sense of seeing far beneath the surface to undercurrents of a deeper reality—as well as to the shifting, introspective interior of Hendrix himself. Projected on a vast scale, across city or skyscape, his image possesses an astral presence. Eyes closed in performance, he becomes an image of contemplation. In her most recent work, where Hatay uses computer technology to explode Hendrix's image into a series of radiant *Mandalas*, the viewer is drawn into the infinite.

Voodoo Child

Nona Hatay's creative process involves a deep, meditative immersion where the boundaries of the intellect are dissolved. Since 1975, when she first began to experiment with the original Hendrix negatives, she has always worked to the sounds of his music. Hatay explains, "I play one song over and over while I create images to illustrate the lyrics and feeling of the music. The room becomes filled with the essence of the piece, and I can translate that into visuals. When people listen to a song and look at the corresponding photo, they say it goes beyond just seeing a picture and becomes a Hendrix experience."

Hatay is far from a single-subject artist. Trained in portraiture by Berta Himler, a leading Bauhaus photographer, she has captured the spirit of many individuals on film. She has created color-expanded photoart series on a broad range of subjects and has published a children's book. But Hendrix is singularly important to Hatay because it was his music and image that first inspired her to break artistic boundaries. Hatay's *PhotoArtWorks*, her monumental interpretive opus of Jimi Hendrix in performance, achieves an unforgettable visualization of the musician as his music.

—Sherry Goodman

Star Spangled Banner

Amplified to match, even surpass, the scale of the modern skyscraper behind him, Hendrix's image here is nonetheless a gentle one. Eyes closed, head tilted back, he sings the familiar, soaring melodies of the national anthem (that closed the Woodstock Festival) in rapt concentration. Hatay projects Hendrix's face across the linear grid of the building in such a way that the vertical architectural lines traverse it; they come to read as guitar strings. Hendrix himself becomes the throat of a guitar, visually merged with his music. Even the flagpole, paralleling these lines, is pulled into the metaphor. And the banner itself flutters away from Hendrix's face as if blown by his breath, by his singing—as if it were the song itself.

Room Full of Mirrors

Here, one image of Hendrix is paired with another, each facing toward the other as do mirrors in the song. Yet Hatay shows Hendrix in each case looking not at himself but, eyes lowered, inward. His raised arm completes the separation between the two. The two images dramatically merge at the level where the guitars sound: here, music plays off itself in kaleidoscopic complexity. The resultant forms in this musical *Room Full of Mirrors* are both crystalline and fragmented like the broken glass of the lyrics and fluid and melting like the love described in the song. The separateness of self from reflection, of self from image above comes together in an endless echo of musical invention.

Belly Button Window

Filling the womb-like nimbus, Hendrix's face glows with an unearthly sheen. This is a night image—thanks to the light-and-dark reversals of the solarization technique—and we perceive the almost tactile light spread thickly across his face as cool and silvery. Gradually we recognize the pools and patterns of light as cloud-edged. It's as if we're looking at the night sky. Hatay transforms the texture of flesh into something ethereal, and the two sides of Hendrix's face—cloud forms drifting apart or together—seem to reach like fingertips across the darkness to keep the image whole.

—Sherry Goodman

JIMI HENDRIX 1942–1970

WHEN JIMI HENDRIX walked across the stage at the Monterey Pop Festival in California during the summer of love, 1967, it was the return of the native. However, the Seattle-born guitarist and former United States Army Screaming Eagle paratrooper had to travel a long way and a long way back in order to harvest the acclaim at home he so richly deserved.

Jimi—born John Allen Hendrix on November 27, 1942—was renamed James Marshall on September 11, 1946. A short time later he picked up his first instrument, the harmonica, but his one true love, the guitar wasn't far off. Jimi has said, "It was the instrument that always seemed to be around. Every house you went to seemed to have one..." Jimi was about 14 when he convinced his father, Al, that their Seattle home needed one as well. He bought Jimi a $5 used acoustic guitar and later recalled, "He wore that thing out. Later on I got him his first electric guitar and I got a sax. I didn't know much about the sax, and he didn't know much about the guitar, so we made quite a bit of noise."

Soon Jimi's affinity for the instrument shone through and as the first wave of the electric guitar washed across the airwaves, his sensitive ears picked up on sounds as diverse as Buddy Holly, B.B. King, Muddy Waters, Eddie Cochran, Elmore James and the magnificent pickers of the Grand Ole Opry.

At seventeen, Jimi left school and joined the 101st Airborne, where he formed an R&B combo, the King Kasuals. The group continued after Jimi's honorable discharge (due to a broken ankle suffered in a parachute jump). His musical trip had begun.

He continued it, contributing as a sideman for a host of R&B greats on the "chittlin' circuit" in the South. Though he learned a lot on that road, he had set his sights higher—he wanted to front his own group.

In pursuit of that goal, Jimi soon entered the New York scene and took first place (winning $25) in an amateur contest at the legendary Apollo Theater in Harlem. Even so, Jimi found the Big Apple a tough town to crack, so he jumped at the chance to join the Isley Brothers for a while and then went on to play for Ike and Tina Turner, King Curtis, Joey Dee, and Little Richard, among others. All the while he was developing his own style and soon returned to New York. Soon after his arrival he attracted the attention of Richie Havens at the Cheetah Club. Richie recalls, "This band goes on, and I hear this wonderful rhythm and blues group. They are kicking. I hear the guitar solo and I turn around to see a guy with the guitar to his face playing notes, and I go 'No, he ain't doing that. How could he be doing that?' It blew my mind.

"I watch the whole damn set. They go into the dressing room and I run back there and I go 'Oh man, where you been all my life?' And he says, 'Aw well, I just left Little Richard in Florida. He fired me and stuff, you know. I'm up here looking for a gig. I got this gig through the union.'

"I said, 'Hey man, you don't need to do this. Period. You don't need to go to no union. You don't need to look for another gig. Get your behind down to Greenwich Village today. Go to the Cafe Wha and tell Manny Roth I told you to come down there. Put your own thing together.'

"Two weeks later, I'm playing at the Cafe A-Go-Go and a friend of mine runs around and says, 'Hey man, you gotta hear this guy around the corner! He's great!' It was Jimmy James and the Blue Flames. That's how it started."

His gigs as the leader of the Blue Flames attracted a following in the coffeehouses of Greenwich Village. His outrageous licks, stage show and style of dress grabbed the ears and eyes of most who crossed his path. But not all were illuminated by Jimi's flame. For example, Andrew Loog Oldham, the Rolling Stones mentor, was left cold. He wrote Jimi off as a wild but unlikely "never-would." Fortunately in August of 1966, Chas Chandler of the disbanding Animals saw more to Jimi than just his flamboyance. He saw talent and plenty of it, and wanted Jimi to come to London to perform.

Chandler knew that Eric Clapton would be floored by Jimi's abilities and promised to introduce Jimi to the British guitar master when Jimi arrived in London. After a little more prodding, Jimi agreed to pull up stakes and head for London. Chandler's prediction about Clapton proved to be quite prescient. When asked about the first time he saw Jimi, Eric reminisced, "It was at the London Polytechnic College. Cream had been going for about three or four months, not very long. Chas Chandler, who I knew from the Animals, came backstage and said he had a young guy with him who would like to jam if that was all right. We were kind of a very liberated band,so we said, 'If he wants to sit in, no problem.' I met this young black kid with funny clothes and big frizzy hair, and he got onstage at one point and he started doing *Killing Floor,* which has got this amazing Hubert Sumlin riff on it, and he knew it. Not only did he know it, but he could take what was already there and make it better. And it blew me away. I was so over the moon and I finally felt like I met someone else that I could talk to and play with on the level that I was involved with the blues. And so he changed my life. In that one short space of time, everything turned upside-down."

Eric's endorsement further convinced Chas that he had indeed found a rare talent. As for Jimi, he was ecstatic. He had neither a band nor any original material. Soon he would have both. Noel Redding responded to an ad in *Melody Maker* seeking a guitarist for an Animals reformation. Chandler convinced him to learn to play the bass and sign on with Jimi. Then Mitch Mitchell nosed out Aynsley Dunbar in the drummer category. Rehearsals began immediately and soon the word of this new group, The Jimi Hendrix Experience, was all over the London rock rumor line. Chas was hard at work behind the scenes booking the group, getting the word out and producing the studio sessions. It should also be pointed out how great a songwriting influence Chas Chandler had on Jimi. He forced Jimi to discipline his creative power and devote it to create three-to-four-minute masterpieces. This allowed him to get the early radio play that later allowed his longer pieces to be heard.

Eric Clapton's early enthusiasm spread to nearly every rock luminary in London, and their presence in support of Jimi made The Experience's shows *the* place to be. Though Mitch and Noel provided a great foundation for the band, the focus was on Jimi. And he made the most of it, playing with his teeth, behind his back, between his legs and while rolling on the floor. His showmanship sometimes overshadowed his amazing technique, but the combination of the two provided the very electricity that British audiences hungered for. Jimi become the toast of London in no time, scoring hits with *Hey Joe* and *Purple Haze*.The Experience album *Are You Experienced* was released in England in May of 1967. By that time, plans were in the works to return Jimi to his homeland.

John Phillips, co-founder of the Mamas and the Papas, had become promoter of the Monterey Pop Festival, which was scheduled to erupt in California during the summer of 1976. At the suggestion of Paul McCartney, who had seen Jimi's explosive version of *Sargent Pepper* in London, Phillips booked The Experience onto the Monterey roster.

It was a stellar choice. The summer of love was in full swing. During those three days of music before thousands of hippie pioneers, peace, love and flowers found a home, a voice, and a national consciousness. On the final night of the festival, Sunday, June 18, the assembled masses were shocked when the Who's *My Generation*, capping a sizzling set, evolved into a free-for-all of destruction as Pete Townsend destroyed his guitar and Keith Moon obliterated his drum kit, while singer Roger Daltrey swung his microphone madly in the thickening smoke generated by the group's onstage explosions. Those in attendance must have thought they had then seen it all. They hadn't.

Jimi Hendrix had been watching in the wings and was determined that he could top what he had just witnessed. He wowed the home crowd with all the magic he possessed. An introduction by Brian Jones cleared the way for one of the most electrically charged shows ever witnessed. Virtually unknown in the States at the start of his set, Jimi had become infamous by its fiery conclusion. Pulling out all the stops, he mesmerized the audience with his playing and his well-honed tricks. Combining sexual abandon with seeming madness, he tore through his set like a man possessed, but always with the audience in mind. During The Experience's closer of the Troggs' *Wild Thing*, Jimi did the unimaginable. He soaked his hand-painted Stratocaster with lighter fluid and set it afire. That image made a lasting impression, though it was one of the few times he took that incendiary approach. Jimi later said, "The times I burned my guitar, it was like a sacrifice. We sacrifice things we love. I love my guitar." The audience seemed somehow in tune with that spirit, but they were still aghast, ecstatic and emotionally drained, pummeled aurally and visually. A star was born that night.

Hendrix soon became the talk of America, just as he had done in England. His musical blitzkrieg next assaulted San Francisco, home of some of the most sophisticated rock fans of the time. After one night at the legendary Fillmore, Jimi rocketed to the top of the bill. Southern California fell a week later. New York collapsed without a fight after an Experience appearance in Central Park on July 5. The U.S. release of *Are You Experienced* added to the acclaim. By the end of 1967, Jimi had added West Germany and Sweden to his empire and he and The Experience were set to release their second album.

In January of 1968 (February in the United States), *Axis: Bold As Love* was released to further critical accolades. The revolutionary techniques used on *Axis* combined Jimi's sounds with the masterful and experimental recording skills of engineer Eddie Kramer. The results are even more amazing when one realizes that what is heard was created on the spot. The canned effects available today still cannot fully capture the sounds of '68.

Ten months later, in spite of an intensive touring schedule, The Experience released *Electric Lady.* It was their most ambitious effort. To begin with, four sides of top-notch material doubled the effort and creative energy required. Secondly, Jimi's songwriting had matured to a new level, both musically and lyrically (At the time,Jimi expressed a particular love for the poetry of e.e. cummings). Third, the production of the album as well as the playing of Jimi and friends reached new heights. The addition of horns, keyboards, and additional percussion stretched the trio concept as far as it could go. Hendrix's personal stamp can be heard all over the album. His influences and his visions were all fused into one package and tied together with his trademark sound. It was nothing short of brilliant. It was also the final studio album Jimi released.

Trouble in The Experience paradise drove a wedge through the trio. Jimi also became a target for conservative paranoia as police and other officials in cities such as Dallas, Tuscaloosa, Toronto, Denver, and Houston took offense at Jimi's choice of music ("The Star Spangled Banner!") or merchandise (a poster featuring two nudes) or his place in the counter-culture. Legal problems, both criminal and civil, caused Jimi to further withdraw into his only fortress—his music.

In many ways, Jimi felt constrained by his partners. True genius does not come very often and the genius of Hendrix as a guitarist and composer needed different outlets and expressions to reach its full potential. He began to play with a number of musicians other than Mitchell and Redding. When Jimi assembled an impromptu line-up on June 22 at the Newport Pop Festival in San Fernando, CA, the result was exciting and very satisfying.

When Noel left the band and was replaced by Billy Cox—Jimi's old army buddy and a former member of the King Kasuals—the Woodstock Music and Arts Fair loomed only a month away.

Hendrix headlined the historic festival with a new, virtually unrehearsed outfit called Gypsys Suns and Rainbows. They headlined the three-day fest, which had spilled over into Monday. Much of the audience had left before this grand finale and many of the stragglers heard only the early portions of Gypsys' set. Jimi played brilliantly at times and his early morning performance of "The Star Spangled Banner" will remain part of rock's mythology.

Jimi continued to move on, and he experimented with new sounds and new players. His next album came with a new cast, The Band of Gypsys, featuring Jimi, Billy Cox and drummer and vocalist Buddy Miles. Their January 1, 1970 show became a recording called simply *Band Of Gypsys.* The funky grooves throughout the album predated a great deal of what was to come during the 70s funk scene.

Meanwhile Jimi was breaking ground on another front. He and his associates had begun constructing his dream studio, Electric Lady. With his first recordings at the Lady, Jimi became the first rock artist to own his means of production. At the same time, creating a state-of-the-art studio in Jimi's image required massive infusions of capital. Much of the profit from his concerts went to pay for construction and other costs.

Fortunately, The Experience had become the largest grossing act of the era. (This was due in part to an innovative concept of self-promotion which is now a rock standard. The Hendrix gang was able to retain 85–90% of gross revenues versus the usual 60% of the day.) They needed nearly every penny to finance Electric Lady's escalating costs. Jimi was very proud of the studio. It was his home and he recorded some of his finest work there, but there was still work to do to complete the studio and more shows were needed to pay for the work.

Many of the 1970 shows, with Cox and Mitchell comprising The Experience's rhythm section, were brilliant. Jimi had moved into new territory musically and Billy and Mitch supported him beautifully. Their recordings at Electric Lady continued as well. A new day was dawning for Jimi and The Experience. Jazz masters such as Miles Davis and Gil Evans had taken notice of Jimi's playing and compositions, and collaborations in that genre had already begun. The future looked bright when Electric Lady's doors officially opened on August 26, 1970. And then it was over.

Jimi died in London on September 18. He left behind a series of recordings and a wealth of stories both true and fantastic. More important, he left behind a guitar revolution as thorough as that of Louis Armstrong on the trumpet or Lester Young on sax. No one who has strapped on a guitar to play rock since Jimi's earliest days has not been touched by his legacy, whether they know it or not. His music lives on. His legend continues. There can only be one Jimi Hendrix. Long may he wave.

—Jym Fahey

THE CONCERT MAY 18,1969

IN 1969, I HAD JUST MOVED to New York City from Switzerland. It was my first year of being a professional photographer. Mostly I worked for underground newspapers photographing musicians in concert. On May 18, I got a call in the morning from one of them, the *New York Review*, to go on assignment to photograph The Jimi Hendrix Experience at Madison Square Garden! It was an unexpected surprise.

Since I had a press pass, I was right next to the stage with a small group of other photographers. It was a little confusing. There was a revolving stage, so that Jimi came and went by and then came back around again. I stayed in one place and got photos of both sides of him as he came and went around. I remember him saying he did not like the revolving stage and would never play there again. He wished his management had told him ahead of time. I thought it sad. I know he liked to make eye contact with some of the audience and fed off the people responding to his music, and on a revolving stage he could not do this.

To make matters worse, fans in the front rows kept flashbulbs popping through the show, even when Jimi asked them to stop. We professional photographers, of course, did not use flash attachments. I remember there was a lot of red lighting which made some of my photos come out too dark. This was my first year as a professional photographer so I am actually amazed I did as well as I did.

Needless to say, it was very loud next to the speakers, and I was almost deaf for 3 days!

People always ask me whether I met Jimi. No, I did not. As I was leaving the concert the backstage guard saw my press pass and let me through. I looked down the hall and knew where Jimi was, but I thought to myself, what will I say, "It was a great show"? I felt I would be just another person disturbing him, so I left. There was a large crowd of women trying to get backstage and they watched in amazement as I turned and walked away.

—Nona Hatay

Forget everything that happened today or yesterday or last night...tonight we'll make our own little world.

—Jimi Hendrix
Madison Square Garden
May 18, 1969

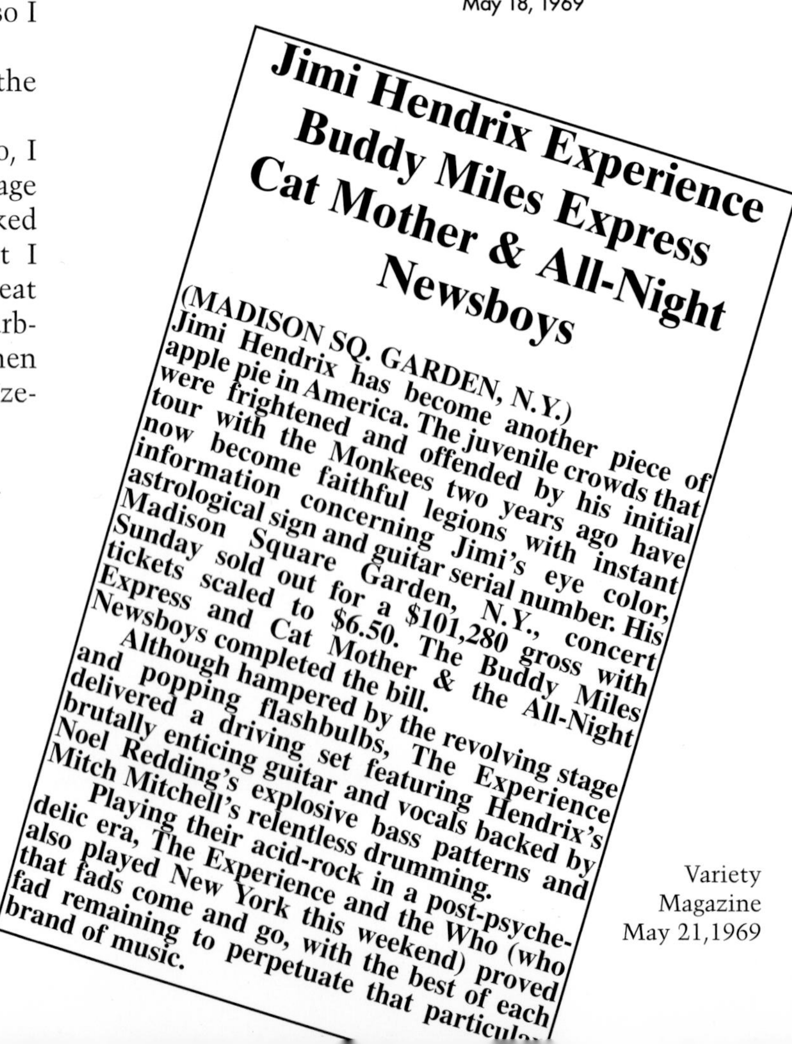

Jimi Hendrix Experience
Buddy Miles Express
Cat Mother & All-Night Newsboys

(MADISON SQ. GARDEN, N.Y.)
Jimi Hendrix has become another piece of apple pie in America. The juvenile crowds that were frightened and offended by his initial tour with the Monkees two years ago have now become faithful legions with instant information concerning Jimi's eye color, astrological sign and guitar serial number. His Madison Square Garden, N.Y., concert Sunday sold out for a $101,280 gross with tickets scaled to $6.50. The Buddy Miles Express and Cat Mother & the All-Night Newsboys completed the bill.

Although hampered by the revolving stage and popping flashbulbs, The Experience delivered a driving set featuring Hendrix's brutally enticing guitar and vocals backed by Noel Redding's explosive bass patterns and Mitch Mitchell's relentless drumming.

Playing their acid-rock in a post-psychedelic era, The Experience and the Who (who also played New York this weekend) proved that fads come and go, with the best of each fad remaining to perpetuate that particul... brand of music.

Variety
Magazine
May 21,1969

I think they should make special buildings, like they make special buildings for restaurants and hotels. They should make special buildings for loud, or whatever you want to call it, electronic rock music. It's fun to play at little funky clubs because that's like a workhouse. It's nice to sweat. I remember we used to play sometimes—even the amplifiers and guitars actually were sweating. Everything is sweating. It seemed like the more it got sweaty, the funkier it got and the groovier. Everybody melted together, I guess! And the sound was kickin' 'em all in the chest. I dig that! Water and electricity! That's what bein' a musician's about—just playing. Playing anywhere. That's why we can play Madison Square Garden and come down and play at the Experience, then go back over and play the Whiskey and then play Hollywood Bowl.

.—Jimi Hendrix

I feel Jimi's plugged into the clouds now. I miss him but I bet he has a new band with John Coltrane, Roland Kirk, Eric Dolphy and other great musicians. I hope he's having a good time.

—Mitch Mitchell

Still now I am completely knocked out by the impact our music has made on the public and the effect it has had on my life.

—Noel Redding

JIMI HENDRIX at Madison Square Garden was one of the first concerts that I attended. At the time I was 18 years old. It was the first and last show that I ever saw with a stage that revolved while the show was going on. I remember being impressed by them setting up the drum kit. They had to nail it to the floor. The amplifiers were all Marshall. There were six stacks of two four-speaker bins with an amp on top. Three stacks on each side of the drums. On a platform outside of the revolving stage were four non-moving sets of horn speaker arrays. The sound system as a whole was tiny by today's standards but back then it was considered loud. Photography was allowed back then at shows. A lot of people had brought cameras with flash attachments. When the room was darkened the flashes started going off. Hendrix started playing but was distracted. After a while I think he made a comment about being sick from the spinning around. A while later he said that the flashes were too much for him. He asked the crowd to take pictures now and to stop for the rest of the night. Well, they took the pictures when he said but they didn't stop. He started jamming on Voodoo Child for quite a long time. His appearance was a little different than I had expected. He had shortened his hair and wore a headband. I thought the mix was good. The big problem was the revolving stage. The sound was great when the stage faced you but that only lasted for a short time. Some people started to walk around the garden in the aisles. That started to get more popular and a lot of people started walking around the garden to keep facing the stage. That's about all I can remember.

—Michael Caruso

Nona Hatay

1970s
BLACK & WHITE EXPERIMENTS

AFTER FIVE OF THE PICTURES I took appeared in the *New York Review*, I put the negatives away. A year and a half later, Hendrix died. I felt very protective of the negatives and didn't print any for five years.

I remember one day in 1975 I was listening to Hendrix's *Voodoo Child* and it seemed to be speaking directly to me. I wanted to be the voodoo child, to go beyond reality into the magical. I remembered the concert and I thought, "How can I put more of the Hendrix energy, electricity and complexity into these photographs?" I started to experiment in the darkroom, playing the Hendrix song I was working on over and over, so that I could put the feelings of the music and lyrics into the pictures. It became an assignment to myself that I worked on intensively for periods of time. Then I'd do other things, like earn a living as a free-lance photographer or work on other photoart series and children's books. Then suddenly I'd have another burst of Hendrix creativity. At times it was a financial sacrifice to work on the project, but it seemed important, even though at the time I had no plans to exhibit, to sell, or even to show anyone what I was doing. I was very private about the whole thing. After awhile, I had a number of pieces finished and wanted to pair them up with their lyrics.

The first book I created was a one-of-a-kind labor of love called *Views of Jimi's Views of Life*. It contained 9 x 13 photographs bound by John Stahl of Evanescent Press, San Francisco, in the fall of 1975. The lyrics were attached opposite each photograph. I felt that it was important to have the lyrics available. I thought of them as poems. And since the pictures were created while listening to the music, lyrics seemed to complete the circle. At this time I had a photography studio and gallery in San Francisco, STUDIO HATAY.

I moved to Three Rivers, Massachusetts the following year. Wanting to continue pairing lyrics and photoart, I thought a limited edition portfolio based on the Hendrix book would be a good idea, though I had no idea how to even start. My father had just died, and I was living a reclusive life in the country. I got a loan, and worked on the project very intensely for a year, producing some of my best work. I eventually finished 15 copies of *The Hendrix Portfolio*.

—Nona Hatay

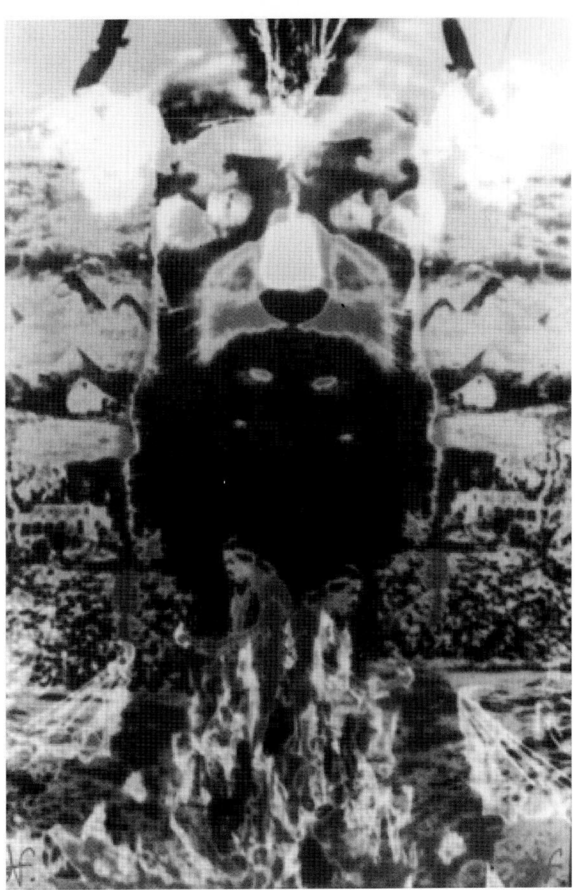

Most of what has been written about Jimi is based on a distorted picture fabricated for the public. It shows the image but not the man, describing the surface but not capturing the spirit behind the music. Most journalists and writers failed to realize the true spiritual core of Jimi and his work—the source he drew all his music and creativity from.

Jimi was not a "wild man." He was an intelligent, natural, shy, and gentle person with a highly developed sensitivity. He saw things with different eyes than most people around him. His perception was more intense than anyone else's. He was a mysterious person at all times, always going into the depth of things, searching, exploring, finding answers, and never standing still. He was a true genius and rebel in his music.

Jimi had the ability to take people through space and time and beyond. His mind and thoughts were full of revolutionary ideas not just about music but also about how to understand and change this world. His final goal was to bring harmony, peace and love to everyone. This was the true purpose in his life as he himself saw it. However, Jimi believed he was just at the beginning of what he set out to achieve. He sacrificed a lot of his personal life to reach his goal, but wasn't given enough time to complete his mission.

Jimi had immense spiritual insight and knowledge. When he spoke to me about this subject, it was like entering a new world full of magic, light, and wonders. This was the world he lived in—the world he regarded as the true reality and the world he wanted to bring into our world, for our planet to become a more spiritual and just place for all of us.

Nona Hatay is one of the rare people who is able to capture Jimi's magic and spirit in her beautiful pictures.

—Monika Dannemann

If you are going to do somebody else's songs, most people do it and say, "Well, this is popular now, we guess we'll do this" but everybody knows that Bob Dylan's *Like a Rolling Stone* isn't popular now. It's a certain respect you might have. You know, you just don't do everybody's songs and if you're going to do them well, like you don't necessarily have to copy it like them. If you really dig the person and really, really dig the song, well then you do it your own way. I like the way we do *Rolling Stone* myself. –Jimi Hendrix 1967

Jimi Hendrix often remarked that Bob Dylan had been one of his major influences. Among other things, he said that Dylan gave him the courage to sing. Hendrix loved Dylan. In tribute, he recorded four Dylan songs over the span of his career. Dylan recently wrote of the improbability of any musician performing his songs well:

> "it's like getting inside of another persons soul . . . my songs are different and i don't expect others to make attempts to sing them."

But Dylan made an exception in the case of Hendrix.

> "he sang them exactly the way they were intended to be sung & played them the same way. he did them the way i would have done them if i was him . . . it's not a wonder to me that he recorded my songs but rather that he recorded so few of them because they were all his."

I love this mutual admiration between great musicians, Bob Dylan and Jimi Hendrix.

—Nona Hatay

The electric church—
that's just a belief that I have. We do use electric guitars and everything is electrified these days, you know, so the belief comes through electricity to the people. That's why we play so loud because it doesn't actually hit through the eardrums like most groups do nowadays. They think well we're going to play loud too and because they're playing loud they get this real shrill sound and it's really hard. We play for our sound to go inside the soul of a person and awake some kind of thing in their mind because there are so many sleeping people.

—Jimi Hendrix

Nona Hatay

Rhythm **&** Blues,

Rock **&** Roll,

Right **&** Wrong,

War **&** Peace,

Love **&** Hate,

Black **&** White,

Jimi Hendrix turned over
all the stones musically,
lyrically and spiritually.
Nona Hatay's PhotoArtWork
captures the **beauty**
and the **spirit**
of this universal man's
many facets.
From **electrifying**
to **flamboyant**,
Jimi's presence is a visual pleasure.
Thank God,
Nona was there at this great time.

—Rosa Lee Brooks A.K.A. Golden Rose

Someday Mystics will discover

what you have uncovered
with your AX/AXIS **BOLD AS LOVE**
and then may we cross that Rainbow Bridge
As Doves...
Space Rock
At
WOODSTOCK
Space Rock
At
Woodstock/ i said

Space Rock
AT
WOODSTOCK

Soaring cosmically within our hearts
and lives.

What bright **Voodoo eyes**

Oh say...did... I...see...
with that hymn to the Republic

Machine gun shuttered
My
What bright **VooDoo eyes/**
you have...

—Emikan Sudan

Nora Hatay

Music is a safe type of high. It's more the way it's suppose to be. That's where highness came from anyway. It's nothing but rhythm and motion.
–Jimi Hendrix

from the middle of a tomb whose lights
burn only for survival . . .
our tired bodies finally understands our
always ~~[illegible]~~ hearts
Beating

Meet me in the Country
Meet me in the Country
the City's breath is getting
away too evil to breathe •
Meet us in the Country
~~[illegible]~~ Leave the pigs and
rats in the City —
Under the Gypsy Sun, we
All will ~~[illegible]~~ clearly Reach the ~~[illegible]~~ Grace
of ~~[illegible]~~ living . . . to Give and Recieve Love and with EASE •

Be Beat

2. We'll Dance to the drums
of the ~~[illegible]~~ ~~Open~~ OPEN Life . . . .
Love is the Rythym of ~~[illegible]~~
man and Wife . . .

Drifting
On a sea of forgotten teardrops
On a lifeboat
Sailing for
Your love
Sailing home

Drifting
On a sea of old heartbeats
On a lifeboat
Sailing for
Your love
Sailing home

—Jimi Hendrix

Jimi! Jimi! Jimi! What can I say? There was no one like you before your incarnation; there has been no one since. Jimi's music and sense of freedom helped to shape my own expressions of creativity and my personal determination to be authentic.

Nona's visual interpretations of Hendrix never cease to amaze me with their beauty and power. It's as if the souls of the two artists meld into a oneness that is beyond the sum of the two. Over the years I have come to relate to Hendrix and Hatay as something of a single entity. I cannot think of Nona without also thinking of Jimi. Nor am I able to think of Jimi without holding thoughts of Nona in the same mind-heart space.

Eternal gratitude to Ms. Hatay on the mastery of her artistry, and for her willingness to bring even greater beauty to the already quite beautiful Jimi.

—Rev. Carlos W. Anderson

The Hendrix Portfolio

Lyrics - Jimi Hendrix
- Original Photographs -
Nona Hatay
Introduction - John McLaughlin
Calligraphy - Joan Saalfield

published by Studio Hatay

Preface

This portfolio is a tribute to the music and essence of Jimi Hendrix.

The portfolio's conception dates back to my asking "Why can't my photographs taken in concert reverberate with the same excitement I feel from listening to Hendrix's music?"

Answering the question took four years of experimentation. Immersing myself in his music, I constantly revised and refined my photographic impressions, inspired by the intensity of the electric sounds and the variety of Jimi's many moods. The images in the lyrics are also reflected in these photographs, while the energy of his words are interpreted in the calligraphy based on his handwriting.

For this Hendrix experience I have included a tape with the corresponding songs for your listening pleasure while viewing the portfolio

Nona Hatay 9/7/78

Freedom
If 6 was 9
Up from the Skies
Astro man
Purple Haze
Roomful of Mirrors

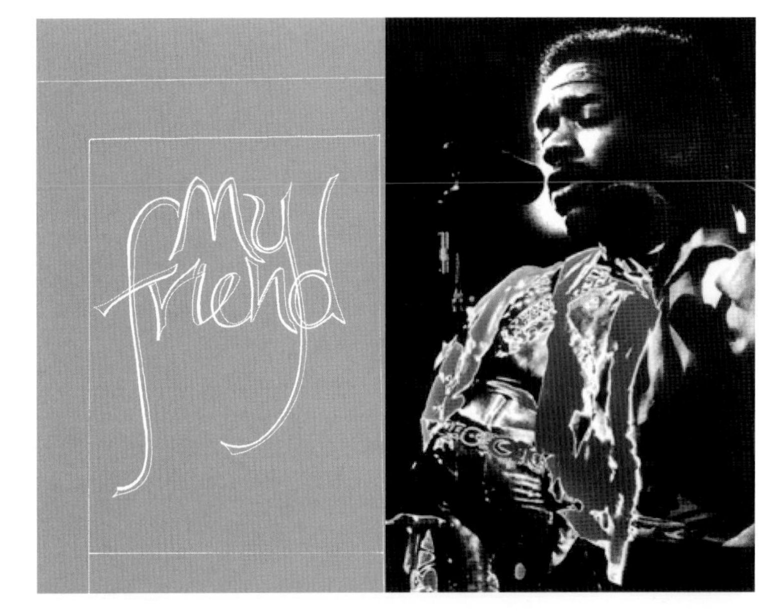

As a photoartist, Hatay is keeping alive the spirit of Hendrix the experimentalist. Hatay's photography is dialectical: the experimental techniques she uses equal the intensity of the sounds of the electric guitar. The photographs are multiple-printed positive and negative images. She improvises, weaving photographs in various combinations. This approach creates an explosion of Hendrix images never seen before. When you listen to the Hendrix tape enclosed in the *Portfolio* and look at the photographs, you will experience them in an expanded way. The photographs appear like musical notes on a score, ascending and descending, moving in and out, rocking back and forth to the beat of *Bold as Love*, *Purple Haze*, *Room Full of Mirrors*, and *Voodoo Chile*. There is no doubt that Hatay has introduced a new art form to the world of music. The photographic genius of Hatay, like the brilliance of Hendrix, is no longer dreaming of freedom—it is now a reality.

—Ari Freemen Cohen

In 1978, Nona Hatay designed and produced the *Hendrix Portfolio*, a conceptual creation linking the music, words and visuals of Jimi Hendrix with an introduction written by John McLaughlin. A limited edition of 100 copies was planned. 15 were completed in 1978; 85 are yet to be produced.

The portfolio contains 10 original experimental photographs, each inspired by a hendrix composition. Each photograph is paired with its corresponding lyrics. The lyrics are written in a calligraphy specially designed by Joan Saalfield to resemble Hendrix's handwriting. Designed by bookbinder David Bourbeau, the portfolio box contains a casette tape of the ten songs.

Ideally, one listens to the music while viewing the pictures and reading the lyrics.

1980s
COLOR EXPANSION

AFTER THE PRODUCTION of the Hendrix Portfolio, I took a break for a few years. In 1983–4, I put together my first book, *Jimi Hendrix: the Spirit Lives On...* The black & white photographs and *PhotoArtWorks* were accompanied by texts reflecting on the spirit of Hendrix. Then I took another break for several years. I was inspired to paint directly on my black & white photoart in the mid 80s, and explored various media. At first I used oil paint, which created realistic effects. Wanting brighter colors, I tried inks and acrylic. I liked the results because they gave a more surrealistic feel to the work. I've always loved black & white photography, its form and lighting, and its reality. Combining all this with the fantasy of color gave me great pleasure, not only in creating my Hendrix work but in other series of *PhotoArtWorks* as well.

In 1987, on vacation in Florida, I heard of the death of Andy Warhol. It somehow affected me, making me more uninhibited in my work. I started using wax crayons and became much more adventurous. I scribbled on photos using very bold colors and felt I captured Hendrix's wildness even more strongly. I liked breaking the rules. I also played with xerox art, painting on black & white copies using glitter and collage, which was great fun.

In 1988, I gave birth to my son. I thought once again that I'd never print or paint any more Hendrix pieces.

—Nona Hatay

Nona Hatay '87

BOLD AS LOVE

ANGER HE SMILES, TOWERING, IN SHINY METALLIC PURPLE ARMOR
QUEEN JEALOUSY-ENVY WAITS BEHIND HIM
HER FIRE GREEN GOWN SNEERS AT THE GRASSY GROUND
BLUE ARE THE LIFE-GIVING WATERS, TAKING FOR GRANTED,
THEY QUIETLY UNDERSTAND.
ONCE HAPPY TURQUOISE ARMIES LAY OPPOSITE READY,
BUT WONDERING WHY THE FIGHT IS STILL ON
BUT THEY'RE ALL BOLD AS LOVE
JUST ASK THE AXIS
MY RED SO CONFIDENT,
HE FLASHES TROPHIES OF WAR AND RIBBONS OF EUPHORIA
ORANGE IS YOUNG, FULL OF DARING
BUT VERY UNSTEADY FOR THE FIRST GO ROUND
YELLOW IN THIS CASE,IS NOT SO MELLOW,
IN FACT I'M TRYING TO SAY IT'S FRIGHTENED LIKE ME
AND ALL OF THESE EMOTIONS OF MINE KEEP HOLDING ME
FROM GIVING MY LIFE
TO A RAINBOW LIKE YOU.
BUT I'M BOLD AS LOVE
JUST ASK THE AXIS HE KNOWS EVERYTHING.

—JIMI HENDRIX

Jimi Hendrix's remarkable performance of his early composition, *Foxy Lady*, at the Isle of Wight Festival embodied the tensions he increasingly drew on in his all-too-brief career. Jimi's palette of sound was always full, rich, and interesting. But here, Jimi utilized an even wider range of materials than usual, bringing harsh abrasive tones, dissonant intervals, radio interference, and pure silence into the structure of his music.

Jimi began *Foxy Lady* with the single pitch of an F# that rang on and on, magically sustained through exquisitely controlled feedback. The note built and built in volume, without any rhythmic or harmonic substructure from the drums or bass. Jimi, capable of incredible speed, intentionally lingered on one single note for more than 40 seconds. He showed us not melody, not harmony, not rhythm—but *tone*, pure electric and energetic sound. Here, Jimi pushed past time, transcending it and showing us the *shape* of the note; the color; the meaning; the quality of the *interior* of his music.

That quality is ineffable—it can neither be analyzed nor explained. It is meaningful, powerful, and evocative, intimately bound up with tension; at once creative, fertile, chaotic, frightening, and beautiful.

Jimi's music is all-inclusive, and it is this inclusiveness, this ability to transform *all* raw materials into beauty, that makes him a consummate artist. Jimi included harmony and dissonance, joy and pain, the old and the new, clarity and distortion, creation and destruction, love, and something grittier in this song—and hints at all these things in his first note. But Jimi's artistry is not a crucible; the elements in it do not melt and merge, but struggle and resist each other. This music is urgent, restless, and vital—and so is Jimi's spirit.

9/22/82

Dear Ms Hatay;

I am Sorry To have Taken so long To answer your letter, I Try To answer each fan personally & it can become quite a job, but I enjoy it. It really does my heart proud, To Know That so many people still remember Jimi, & are inspired by his music. I see That your quite The photographer, your work is very, very good. I've always been enterested in photography but couldn't Take The Time To get into it, right now my Thing is golf, I'm an out-doors-man, & when The weathers nice, That's where I'll be, out of doors.

Maybe one of These days we will meet in person, in The mean Time, Thank you ever so much for The photos & Take care I send my best regards To you.

Sincerely

James A. Hendrix

MAY THIS BE LOVE

WATERFALL, NOTHING CAN HARM ME AT ALL,

MY WORRIES SEEM SO VERY SMALL,

WITH MY WATERFALL.

I CAN SEE MY RAINBOW CALLING ME,

THROUGH THE MISTY BREEZE

OF MY WATERFALL.

SOME PEOPLE SAY DAYDREAMING'S FOR THE LAZY-MINDED FOOLS,

WITH NOTHING ELSE TO DO.

SO LET THEM LAUGH, LAUGH AT ME,

SO JUST AS LONG AS I HAVE YOU

TO SEE ME THROUGH, I HAVE NOTHING TO LOSE,

LONG AS I HAVE YOU.

WATERFALL, DON'T EVER CHANGE YOUR WAYS.

COME WITH ME FOR A MILLION DAYS,,

OH MY WATERFALL.

—JIMI HENDRIX

©Nona Hatay

1983. . . (A MERMAN I SHOULD TURN TO BE)

HOORAY, I AWAKE FROM YESTERDAY,
ALIVE BUT THE WAR IS HERE TO STAY
SO MY LOVE, CATHERINA AND ME
DECIDE TO TAKE OUR LAST WALK THROUGH THE NOISE TO THE SEA.
NOT TO DIE BUT TO BE REBORN
AWAY FROM LANDS SO BATTERED AND TORN
FOREVER.

OH SAY, CAN YOU SEE IT'S REALLY SUCH A MESS
EV'RY INCH OF EARTH IS A FIGHTING NEST,
GIANT PENCIL AND LIPSTICK TUBE SHAPED THINGS
CONTINUE TO RAIN AND CAUSE SCREAMING PAIN
AND THE ARCTIC STAINS FROM SILVER BLUE TO BLOODY RED
AS OUR FEET FIND THE SANDS AND THE SEA
IS STRAIGHT AHEAD (STRAIGHT UP AHEAD).

WELL, IT'S TOO BAD THAT OUR FRIENDS CAN'T BE WITH US TODAY
"THE MACHINE THAT WE BUILT,
IT WOULD NEVER SAVE US" THAT'S WHAT THEY SAY
(THAT'S WHY THEY'VE NOT COME UP WITH US TODAY)
THEY ALSO SAID "IT'S IMPOSSIBLE
FOR A MAN TO LIVE AND BREATHE UNDER WATER FOREVER,"
THAT WAS THEIR MAIN COMPLAINT.

(AND THEY ALSO THREW THIS IN MY FACE, THEY SAID:)
"ANYWAY, YOU KNOW GOOD AND WELL IT WOULD BE BEYOND THE WILL OF
GOD AND THE GRACE OF THE KING."

SO MY DARLING AND I MAKE LOVE IN THE SAND
TO SALUTE THE LAST MOMENT EVER ON DRY LAND
OUR MACHINE, IT HAS DONE ITS WORK, PLAYED ITS PART WELL
WITHOUT A SCRATCH ON OUR BODIES WE BID IT FAREWELL.
STARFISH AND GIANT FOAMS GREET US WITH A SMILE
BEFORE OUR HEADS GO UNDER WE TAKE A LAST LOOK AT THE KILLING NOISE
OF THE OUT OF STYLE, THE OUT OF STYLE. . . OUT OF STYLE.

—JIMI HENDRIX

I USED TO LIVE IN A ROOM FULL OF MIRRORS
ALL I SEEN WAS ME
I USED TO LIVE IN A ROOM FULL OF MIRRORS
ALL I SEEN WAS ME
WELL I CAN'T STAND IT NO MORE
SO I SMASHED THE MIRRORS
AND SET ME FREE . . .

—JIMI HENDRIX

IF 6 WAS 9

YEAH, SING A SONG

IF THE SUN REFUSE TO SHINE,
I DON'T MIND, I DON'T MIND.
IF THE MOUNTAINS FELL IN THE SEA,
LET IT BE, IT AIN'T ME.
ALRIGHT, 'COS I GOT MY OWN WORLD TO LOOK THROUGH
AND I AIN'T GONNA COPY YOU.

NOW IF 6 TURNED OUT TO BE 9
I DON'T MIND, I DON'T MIND.
ALRIGHT, IF ALL THE HIPPIES CUT OFF ALL THEIR HAIR,
I DON'T CARE, I DON'T CARE.
DIG, 'COS I GOT MY OWN WORLD TO LIVE THROUGH
AND I AIN'T GONNA COPY YOU.

WHITE COLLARED CONSERVATIVE FLASHING DOWN THE STREET,
POINTING THEIR PLASTIC FINGER AT ME,
THEY'RE HOPING SOON MY KIND WILL DROP AND DIE,
BUT I'M GONNA WAVE MY FREAK FLAG HIGH—HIGH,
WAVE ON, WAVE ON.

FALL MOUNTAINS, JUST DON'T FALL ON ME.
GO AHEAD ON MR. BUSINESSMAN, YOU CAN'T DRESS LIKE ME.

GET ON DREAMIN',
STRIKE'S ON FURTHER.
NOBODY WILL KNOW WHAT I'M TALKING ABOUT.
I GOT MY OWN LIFE TO LIVE
I WANT US NOT TO DIE, OR JUST HALF OF YOU TO DIE.
SO LET ME LIVE MY LIFE
THE WAY I WANT TO

SING ON BROTHER,
PLAY ON DRUMMER.

—JIMI HENDRIX

TOW AWAY ZONE
NO PARKING

UP FROM THE SKIES

I JUST WANT TO TALK TO YOU—I WON'T DO YOU NO HARM
I JUST WANT TO KNOW ABOUT YOUR DIFFERENT LIVES
ON THIS HERE PEOPLE FARM
I HEAR YOU HAVE YOUR FAMILIES
LIVING IN CAGES TALL AND COLD
AND SOME STAY THERE AND DUST AWAY PAST THE AGE OF OLD
IS THIS TRUE?
PLEASE LET ME TALK TO YOU
I JUST WANT TO KNOW ABOUT THE ROOMS BEHIND YOUR MINDS
DO I SEE A VACUUM THERE OR AM GOING BLIND?
OR IS IT JUST REMAINS OF VIBRATIONS AND ECHOES LONG AGO
THINGS LIKE "LOVE THE WORLD" AND "LET YOUR FANCY FLOW"
IS THIS TRUE? PLEASE LET ME TALK TO YOU
LET ME TALK TO YOU
I HAVE LIVED HERE BEFORE THE DAYS OF ICE
AND OF COURSE THIS IS WHY I AM SO CONCERNED
AND I COME BACK TO FIND
THE STARS MISPLACED
AND THE SMELL OF A WORLD THAT HAS BURNT
(WELL MAYBE IT'S JUST A CHANGE OF CLIMATE)
I CAN DIG IT, I CAN DIG IT BABY—I JUST WANT TO SEE
SO WHERE DO I PURCHASE MY TICKET,
I WOULD JUST LIKE TO HAVE A RINGSIDE SEAT
I WANT TO KNOW ABOUT THE NEW MOTHER EARTH
I WANT TO SEE AND HEAR EVERYTHING

—JIMI HENDRIX

Nona Hatay

PURPLE HAZE

PURPLE HAZE
ARE IN MY BRAIN,
LATELY THINGS
DON'T SEEM THE SAME,
ACTIN' FUNNY,
BUT I DON'T KNOW WHY,
'SCUSE ME
WHILE I KISS THE SKY.

—JIMI HENDRIX

His guitar was like an extension of his soul. It wasn't even a guitar, or notes, or music...it was just him. He just projected Jimi Hendrix.

—Johnny Winter

JIMI DEFIED
EVERYTHING PEOPLE WERE DOING
AT THE TIME. HE BROKE ALL THE RULES
AND MADE IT WORK. HE WAS ORIGINAL.
JUST FANTASTIC! HIS STUFF IS SUPER.
I KNOW IT IS SUPER.

—MR. JAMES BROWN

The man Jimi Hendrix was a serious magic person.

Jimi's music impressed me by his second L.P. and then I had the opportunity to see him play and to jam on several occasions. He was very interesting to play with because of the way he kept time and the way I kept time. He was a very accomplished musician. I really enjoyed hanging with him and I really have a lot of respect for him because he was a genuine person. He was really a phenomenal person.

I felt often that people really didn't give him enough room. One of the things that saddens me was that his really open nature invited that kind of thing. He never wanted to hurt anyone's feelings, that was one of the things that was really big about him. I could really see that, but I could also see it was a double-edged sword. He didn't want all that and people would stay on and on and on and on, and eventually that made it really tough on him. He related to everybody. He was a basic person. I certainly enjoyed all the times I was with him. One time, Buddy Miles called and said "Jimi's in town" and we went over and it was amazing—all the people—there was the man cornered in the room, and he was like a panther moving around everybody, trying to keep everybody cool. But he had that kind of thing that people wanted to be touched by him and then they were like "O.K.—I've touched the hem of his garment, I'm saved!" ...that kind of scene. It was amazing. But it was just his way with people and the type of friendliness he exposed people to and was able to give was something that is very important and I never forgot that. I always thought about him and wondered how he was doing, 'cos I'd read things in the newspapers but you'd have to read lines in between the lines to know what was really going on.

As to the music, the things that I like about it, I mean the man was way ahead of his time—way ahead. He got some sounds out of his instrument that they are still trying to get out. A lot of people didn't really get to hear him or understand what he was doing. He did something that I don't think I'll see anyone come along and do in my lifetime.

I think he was a highly spiritual person. Particularly since he is a Sagitarius. Sagitarius has a real interesting play going on between the forces of evil and the forces of light. Often times he would come in on that level—and people, just to get a piece of him, would drag him down in the hole and try to alter his consciousness, one way or another. He worked between that and he always seemed to win, as far as I'm concerned, in terms of the music. There's nothing like it. I come to a point where I'm stuck as to what to say. I just want to put on the music to listen 'cos that's the only way really, to get the true feeling of that type of genius. The man Jimi Hendrix, was a serious magic person.

—Taj Mahal

Nona Hatay

HENDRIX' COMET

Oh radiant joy, sun spun laughs
Fiery rays wisdom words weave
Oh friend of mine, friend of man
So good to feel you close to heart
So good to feel you close at hand
Red ink spilling, hands tilling, fields
Battle torn, dying—
Fiery vital seed implant
Amongst friendship's furrowed crossing
Where time as space as Purple Haze
Beckons spirits love divining
Flowing gently across the stage
Winged Hendrix backstage dancing
Pictures flashing, wheels rolling
Oxide memory tracks—
Hold the fire whilst thee can
In earth-born Kingdom Halls—
Illuminate paths for fools wild wanderings,
Beckon the trumpets call—
Give to all that come in hunger
The promise of my land—
Spectacle lights, star dark lights
Blazing comets, judgement thunder—
Give to all who would uncover
The promise of my hand—
Yea Jimi, yea Nona

—Max Drake

There are a lot of things you have to sacrifice. It all depends on how deep you want to get into whatever your gig is. Whatever you're there for. So like the deeper you get into it the more sacrifices you have to do, maybe even on your personality or your outward this and that. I just dedicate my whole life to this whole art. You have to forget about what other people say. If it's art or anything else, whatever you really, really dig doing, you have to forget about what people say about you sometimes. Forget about this or forget about that—when you're supposed to die or when you're supposed to be living. You have to forget about all these things. You have to go on and be crazy. That's what they call craziness. Craziness is like heaven. Once you reach that point of where you don't give a damn about what everybody else is saying you're goin' toward heaven. The more you get into it, they're goin' to say, "Damn, that cat's really flipped out. Oh, he's gone now." But if you're producin' and creatin', you know, you're gettin' closer to your own heaven. That's what man's trying to get to, anyway. —Jimi Hendrix

Nona Hatay

IMMORTAL IDOL

A*M*E*N

When you put on your coat

& started down the stairs

how I thought:

No, he can't leave like that

Then you turned the mirror's

corner, walking into cool drifts

of absolute reverie

O Poet of the averted glance

& the steel string,

seeking your own image

in the butterfly wing of sleep,

an empty airplane falls

in flames

& you, game for any fling,

rise above the living by virtue

of your sound

which is everlasting!

Poem for Jimi Hendrix
10-year anniversary of Life-in-Death
Paradiso (Amsterdam) Sept. 18, 1980

—Ira Cohen

Reverberant

clarion

call

transcending

space & time

pointing towards

our destiny

of

unfolding

evolutionary

potential.

—John C. Dubberstein

Nona Hatay

JIMI MAY SEEM JUST AN IMAGE IN OUR PICTURE FRAME, BUT HE IS THE LIGHT THAT HAS SHINED ON US ALL.

—SEAN CINEMAIE

One of the most important things Jimi Hendrix gave me was the courage to try new ideas, to allow myself to make mistakes and to keep going through the process, the chaos, into the next level of new creation from the unknown. The experimental photographs that happened in this way are my favorites—a surprise for me, not an idea made visual, but a spontaneous gift from the combination of skill and error. Jimi did this with his use of feedback, usually considered a technical mistake, something to be avoided at all costs. He allowed the mistake, molding and creating it, into a beautiful and powerful part of his music. This is best demonstrated in his *Star Spangled Banner* and in his live concert recordings.

—Nona Hatay

The thing I love is mistakes, because we've come to a point in the arts and music where that's where the new things come from—from overt mistakes. And then knowing how to get out of those mistakes—this is what inprovisation is all about. —Felix Pappalardi 1969

His first number, *Stone Free,* (at Downing Stadium on Randall's Island, New York on July 17, 1970) ended with Jimi's amps picking up a local news radio station which we all thought he did on purpose. During one solo Jimi held his guitar with his right hand, straight out, and played the most incredible lead with his other hand at his side. It seemed to be impossible. When he finished his show, Jimi threw his guitar on the stage, which continued to feedback while he exited into a limousine and was gone. The audience hadn't even started clapping, his guitar was still screaming feedback on the stage. —Larry Blumenstein

Of

everything

you came,

and never

went away.

Unknown colours,

but deep

from soul.

Your voice

is still,

everywhere.

—Lars Skanberg

First saw him at the Peppermint Lounge
long beautiful fingers
flamboyant
years later at the Fillmore
extraordinary music
sensuous electrifying new
the consummate artist.

—Norman Weisberg

electric lady studios
52 west 8 street
Nona Hatay

F. U. N. K.

I'm going to tell you
about a MAN
F. U. N. K.
I'm going to tell you
about a MAN
He had a lot of feeling
Aw . . . in his hands
His name was
Jimi Hendrix
Jimi Hendrix
Aw . . . was his name
He could make that
Aw. . . guitar walk. . .
He could make that
Aw. . . guitar talk now. . .
He could make that
Guitar
Sing–ing
Jimi he could make it do
Anything
Anything
Jimi yes he could
He could
He could make it do
Make it do anything
Anything
He used to say
Foxy Lady
He used to say
Oh Betty Oh Betty
I'm going to get you now. . .
F. U. N. K.

—Betty Davis

BACH, HANDEL AND ORCHESTRAL MUSIC

Hendrix always appreciated classical music, and was planning on learning how to write music so he could work with a full orchestra. He enrolled in the Julliard School of Music just before he died. This certainly would have been an interesting direction for his music.

There's a story about Hendrix when he was living next door to Handel's residence on Brook Street in London. Jimi and his girlfriend Kathy Etchingham made special events out of listening to Handel's Messiah and Water Music by candlelight. Jimi was very moved by the music and felt very close to the composer.

The story became a news item when some people wanted to put a commemorative plaque for Hendrix on Handel's house.

—Nona Hatay

Some people need to be really, really respected. See, these are classical composers. People really have to start learning the value of things as they're living today. As things are happening at a particular time, the people in that particular time don't really know the value of it until it dies off. —Jimi Hendrix

I've always said that one day Jimi Hendrix will be placed in the same category as Handel, Beethoven, Mozart and others but I envisioned that it would be at least 50 to 100 years before his genius was publicly exhorted. Now I see my vision is correct. —Billy Cox

I like Handel and Bach. Handel and Bach is like homework type of thing. You can't hear it with friends all the time. You have to hear some things by yourself. You can listen to anything that turns you on or that takes you for a ride. People want to be taken somewhere. —Jimi Hendrix

Unfortunately we'll never see what would have happened if Hendrix had played with Miles Davis, John McLaughlin, or Gil Evans. That was on the drawing board when he died and that would have been an amazing project. And I believe he would have done orchestral interpretations of his music complete with feedback and everything. "Trumpets and violins can be heard in the distance . . ." —Vernon Reid

I'd like to take a six-month break and go to a school of music. I want to learn to read music, be a model student and study and think. I'm tired of trying to write stuff down and finding I can't. I want a big band. I don't mean three harps and fourteen violins, I mean a big band, full of competent musicians that I can conduct and write for. —Jimi Hendrix

Nora Hatay

What's happening is, you,
we, we have all these different senses.
We've got eyes, nose, you know,
hearing, taste and feeling and so forth.
Well, there's a sixth sense that's comin' in.
Everybody has their own name for it,
but I call it Free Soul. And that's more
into that mental kind of thing.
That's why everything is beyond the eyes now.
The eyes only carry you so far out.
You have to know how to develop
other things that will carry you
further and more clear.
That's why the fastest speed . . .
what's the fastest speed you can think of?
They say the speed of light is the fastest thing—
that's the eyes—but then there's
the speed of thought which is beyond that.
You can get on the other side of this theme in
a matter of thinking about it, for instance.

—Jimi Hendrix

L'AGENDA

DES ACTIVITES CULTURELLES DE LA FNAC

NEW-AGE

JIMI'S BACK

PR. SCHWARTZENBERG

CIE ROYAL DE LUXE

LE JAZZ ET LA FNAC : NOCES DE CUIVRES!

fnac

PARIS ET SA RÉGION

SEPTEMBRE 90

PARIS, FRANCE

In the spring of 1990, Yazid Manov, a young man from Paris, called me in Massachusetts. Yazid had corresponded with me for several years about Hendrix and he wanted to know when I was coming to Paris. I said, rather as a joke, whenever I get an offer to exhibit there. Two weeks later he called me—"I have your exhibit set up, they'll fly you over. Now we can finally meet!" From this start he went on to create a most fantastic week-long Hendrix festival with exhibits, movies, music, and a tribute concert at the Olympia Theater.

It was wonderful, the appreciation the French people gave my work—especially the black & white experimental pieces. They would stand in front of a piece for 15 minutes or more, studying every detail. It made me happy to have their respect, and I finally understood why many artists and musicians who have not been accepted elsewhere end up in Paris. They do treat artists well! I was interviewed on every TV and radio station and was treated like a queen. I felt this was my "15 Minutes Of Fame."

Feeling very honored and satisfied, I made a career change into health care and the healing arts. Once again I thought I'd never print or paint another Hendrix piece, and I didn't—until 1993.

Never say never! —Nona Hatay

"JIMI'S BACK" IN PARIS—ETES-VOUS EXPERIENCED?

As of now, Paris is the capital of Electric Ladyland. It has to be, ever since a prestigious week-long festival, "Jimi's Back," was held in the "City of Light" to commemorate the 20th anniversary of the passing away of James Marshall Hendrix. Organized by Yazid Manou, with a lot of press coverage on radio and TV, the festival's events took place in different locations all over Paris. Gallery FNAC in Montparnasse featured a photoart exhibition by the well-known photographer/artist Nona Hatay, along with an opening party and concert on September 14 by an American group, the Angel Reca Band (Angel Reca on guitar, Dave Bynoe on bass, and Ramone Isaacs on drums). There was an evening of Jimi Hendrix movies, and, on several nights, jam sessions in clubs all over the city. At FNAC on the 18th there was an information forum with Noel Redding, Caesar Glebbeek and Nona Hatay. The highlight of the festival was the tribute concert on the 15th of September. 16 bands filled the famous Paris Olympia Theater to capacity. (Hendrix's first major concert in his musical career was at the Olympia in October 1966 as the opening act for Johnny Haliday.) The whole festival was a great success. **—Ben Valkhoff, September, 1990**

End of 1990
HENDRIX YEAR!
The very first Great Tribute was in PARIS.
Why did I do it?...Nona's fault!!!
My message: "We don't have to wait till tomorrow."
—Yazid Manou

Wild Thing was painted especially for the Paris exhibit, June 1990

LONDON, ENGLAND

JIMI HENDRIX AT THE ROCK CIRCUS

On my way back home after the Paris exhibit, I stopped off in London. Visiting the Rock Circus, I was asked to exhibit my work there. Throughout the months of January and February 1991, Rock Circus presented my *PhotoArtWorks*. They were beautifully displayed beside the life-like wax figure of Jimi Hendrix. The Tussaud Group's Rock Circus is an exciting attraction at Picadilly Circus which features "Bionic Performances by the Immortals of Rock." People are given earphones, and when they approach a figure, the music of that performer starts to play.

It is a wonderful EXPERIENCE! —Nona Hatay

BILLBOARD MURAL TRIBUTE TO JIMI HENDRIX BY CHICO FOR WRANGLER JEANS

Chico is a New York City graffiti artist. He calls his work "City Art." As a child, he was always impressed by large murals on buildings. He went on to create his own works of art in many cities. Most of the famous memorial murals in New York City were created by Chico. His first, painted in 1987, was inspired when a close friend of his was killed.

In 1990, Chico was informed by friends that there was a man in a suit looking for him who wanted to take him to London. Chico paid no attention, and threw the man's number away several times. The man persevered, and they finally met. It turned out that this man was a representative from the Wrangler Jeans company, and had been looking all over the United States for the right mural artist for a special project. After discussions, Chico was commissioned to paint a billboard memorial tribute to Hendrix at Picadilly Circus. Chico was flown to London, put up in style for three weeks, and shown great respect for his talent. Chico had always loved Hendrix, and knew that this would be a good opportunity to "get closer to the man."

I was moved when I saw the billboard, and felt that it was a great piece of art that was keeping the spirit of Hendrix alive. I was inspired to photograph it and to superimpose a few of my Hendrix photographs. The result is yet another union between Jimi and the visual arts.

—Nona Hatay

Imaging by Michael "Bongo" Grabscheid

I find it most appropriate that this book by Nona Hatay be titled *Visions & Reflections* since I've always considered the artistic talents of Jimi Hendrix filled with those two basic qualities. During his earthly existence amongst us, he sought to reflect through his music the spiritual visions which he was able to so profoundly see in his soul's eye. I, like countless millions through the years, have felt those reflections uplift my soul whenever I listen to one of his songs. The heart of the legacy he has given to the world is his unique way of using the gift of spirit, and this will continue to inspire generations in the future. As all our spirits know no boundaries, so Jimi's works have followed the same path through the sands of time.

When I recently viewed Nona's works at a gallery in NYC, I found both her artistic and spiritual "eyes" a direct link to Jimi Hendrix's message. I truly feel she has captured the essence of why Jimi Hendrix has come to be the music legend he is today. He had but one sole purpose throughout his life—to tell those who chose to hear that the light (reflection) of spirit is within each of us, and this creates the vision of a better world that is yet to be. —Lenee Jean Pierre, AKA Lady Supreme

1990s TECHNOART

HAVING COMPLETELY RESISTED using computers until 1993, I am now finding a point of union that is both exciting and inspiring. My first experience with this fusion of art and technology came in a project I did with Michael "Bongo" Grabscheid. I had never touched a computer and felt quite bewildered by the technical challenge. We sat together, and as Bongo introduced me to what computer imaging could do, I started to get ideas—such as rotation (*Mandala*), mirror images (*Angel*), and repetition (*In from the Storm*). Bongo created a beautiful fractal piece called *Invitation* and did some fancy colorization (*Angel, Traveller, Planet Jimi*). What fun we had! The spirit of Jimi was with us, and of course we had the music playing in the background. The resulting series of 11 works became the *Nouveau Retro* series. We exhibited in New York City in September 1993, and the Hard Rock Cafe bought the whole series for their galleries all over the world.

I learned a lot from this encounter. At first I had a massive ego death—it felt as if the experimental photography I had worked so hard to create in the darkroom could be done more quickly and easily on the machine. My 20 years of work seemed to be worth nothing. But, despite the computer's abilities, I soon began to see what it could *not* do. There is a mysterious raw and imperfect quality that I like in my darkroom and hand-painted work—the "humanness." Computer art can be very polished and perfect. Although that is a great quality, I like the combination of perfection and imperfection. Therefore, I like to first create an experimental photo or paint a piece, and then scan it into the computer and continue the creative process. Combining the technical and the human seems like the best of both worlds. I still have a lot to learn and will continue to explore this new direction. —Nona Hatay

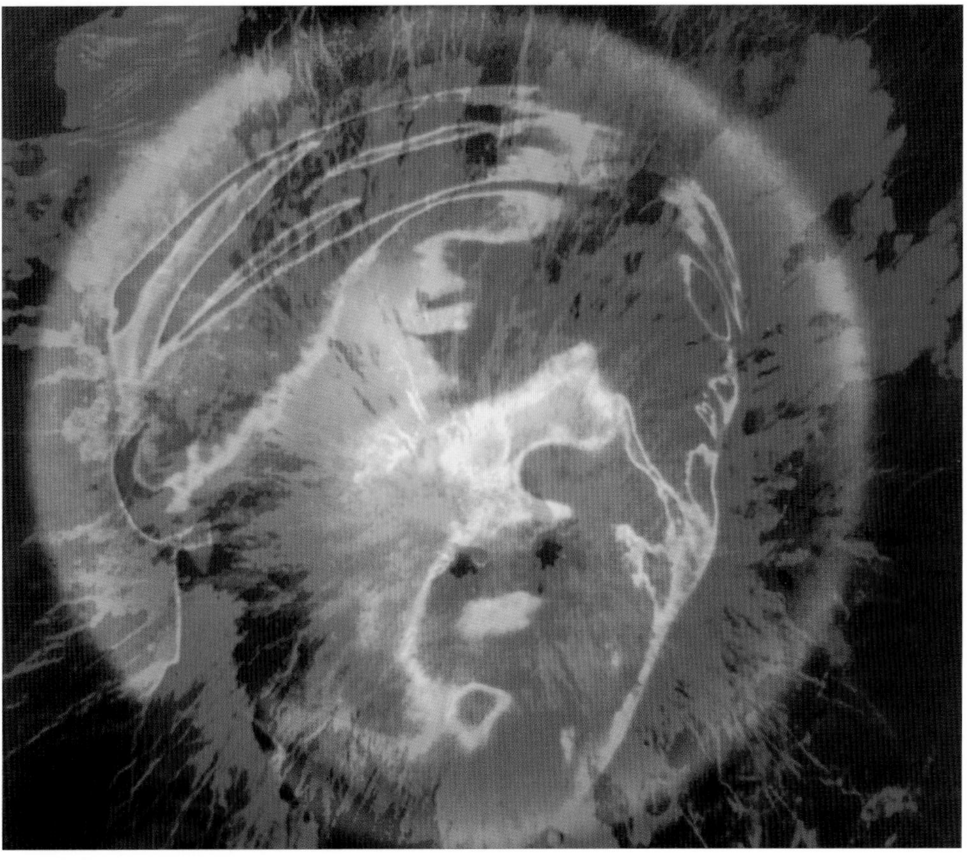

Experimental Photo by Nona Hatay; Imaging by Alice de Young

Hand painted by Nona Hatay. Imaging by Michael "Bongo" Grabsheid.

I started listening to Jimi *(Axis)* just before I started playing with computers. And it's good it happened in that order. Jimi's music made me want to "draw outside the lines." I would always think about ways computers could be used artistically, like recording and mixing music digitally and creating or reworking visual images, but in those days computers didn't do that. Many years later, as I was beginning to dabble with digital photography, I was introduced to Nona Hatay and her ideas about creating a new series of Hendrix art on the computer. Our *Nouveau Retro* series was born of a free-flowing collaboration of artistry and technology. How appropriate that the spirit of Jimi's music provided the inspiration for our playful exploration of computer imagery.

—Michael "Bongo" Grabscheid

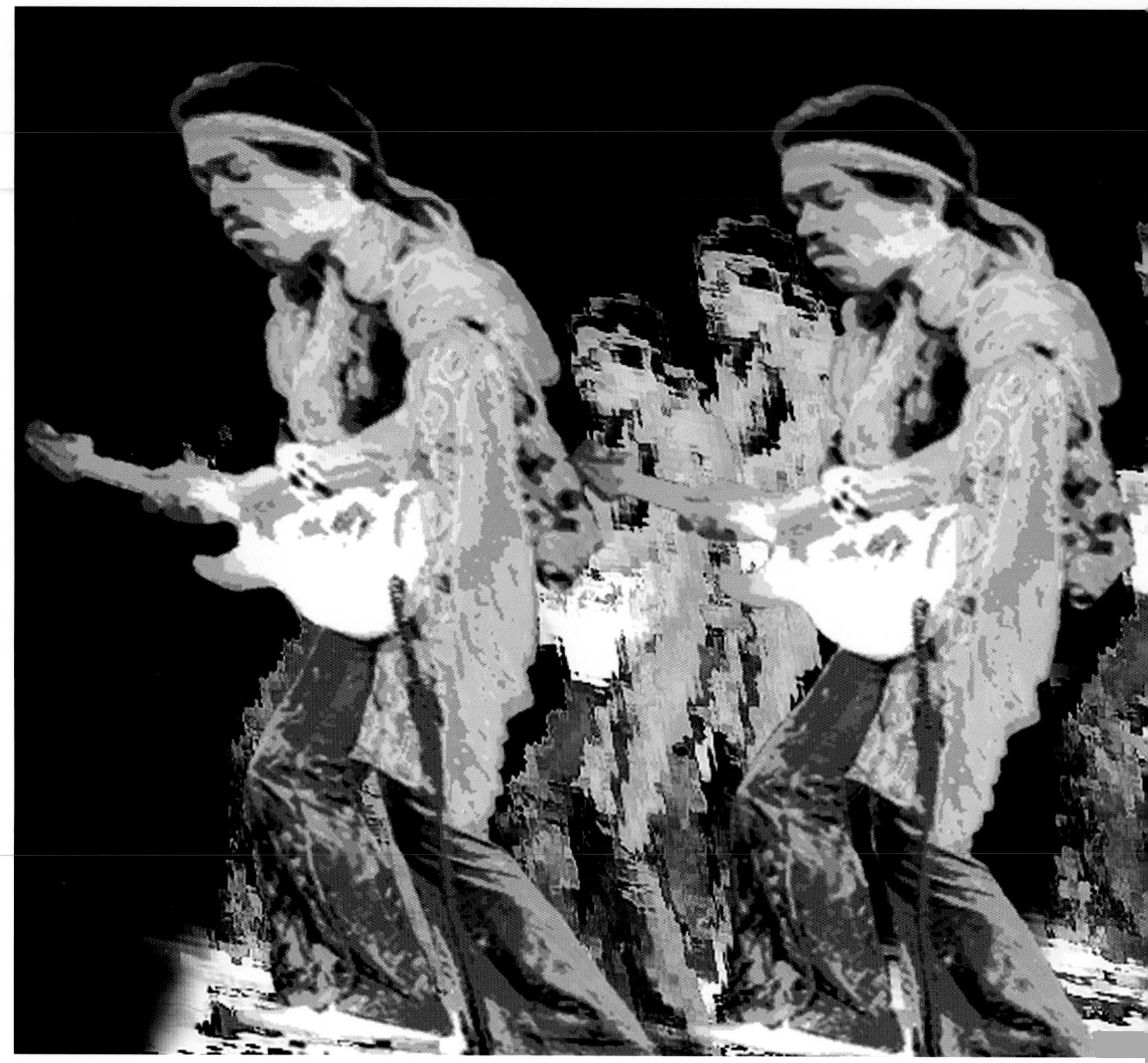

Handpainting and Imaging by Nona Hatay

Once you have the bottom there you can go anywhere. That's the way I believe. Once you have some type of rhythm, like it can get hypnotic if you keep repeating it over and over again. Most of the people will fall off by about a minute of repeating. You do that say for three or four or even five minutes if you can stand it, and then it releases a certain thing inside of a person's head. It releases a certain thing in there so you can put anything you want right inside that, you know. So you do that for a minute and all of a sudden you can bring the rhythm down a little bit and then you say what you want to say right into that little gap. It's somethin' to ride with, you know. You have to ride with something. I always like to take people on trips. That's why music is magic. Already this idea of living today is magic. There's a lot of sacrifices to make. I'm workin' on music to be completely, utterly a magic science, where it's all pure positive. It can't work if it's not positive. The more doubts and negatives you knock out of anything, the heavier it gets and the clearer it gets. And the deeper it gets into whoever's around it. —Jimi Hendrix

I always saw Jimi as a catalyst, through which blues, soul, jazz, rock, folk, psychedelia, pop, poetry, hipness, humour, spirituality, and breathtaking performance could fuse into one man and his guitar. His timelessness was what made him stand out, then and now. This fact made our album *If 60's were 90's* so much easier, for Jimi sounded just as right as part of the future as he did part of the past, riffing through the modern styles of house, funk, ambient, indie and tribal—all of which he had a hand in creating. We tried to use his song approaches to influence us, but in a modern context—almost as a spiritual guide, looking back to his work for inspiration whenever things weren't coming together. It always paid off, but I can never stop wondering what it would have been like had he been around to have a hand in it. People always say it's a cool album, but with Hendrix it would have been mind-blowingly cool!

Nona reads the visual Jimi rather like we tried to read the music of Jimi, by taking the pieces that inspire and channeling them into the present, then onto the future. —Du Kane

When Jimi first played *If Six Was Nine*, the call to the musical revolution was loud and clear. In the two decades since his passing, Hendrix's call has been heeded by countless musicians, but few have channeled his spirit more lovingly and precisely than Du Kane and Luke Baldry. Armed with a sampler, unlimited access to Jimi's back catalogue, and abundantly original musical ideas, the pair bring the legendary guitarist's music straight into the 90s with their group Beautiful People.

If 60s Were 90s, the Surrey, England-based sextet's 18-months-in-the-making Continuum debut, uses Hendrix's often imitated, but never duplicated guitar playing as a springboard for some of the most fascinating head-rock around. With over fifty separate vocal and guitar samples integrated into the album's nine tracks (a chart, contained inside, serves as a guide to the origin of each), *If 60s Were 90s* demonstrates both the timelessness of the original music and the astonishing reach that modern technology has given us.

—Press Release for Beautiful People's CD If 60s were 90s

Experimental PhotoArt and Imaging by Nona Hatay

A lot of people is askin' about why is **bright colors** come along with rock. I mean is this part of it? It's not hiding. A lot of people say, "Oh, there goes a person with a poster. You know, he's wearin' different posters in his face." You say, "Well, dig it, man, you know somebody's got to be the clown." Which is a magician, for instance. Somebody's got to be this and that. And like, the **bright colors**, they're always goin' to be there with our music. —Jimi Hendrix

There's so much I want to do—I want to get **color** into music. I'd like to play a note and have it come out a **color**. . . in fact I've got an electrician working on a machine to do that right now.

—Jimi Hendrix to the British Press, 1966

Experimental PhotoArt and Imaging by Nona Hatay

Jimi and I once talked about astral travel and we came up with the idea of space brothers; beings from two different worlds who would, as a means of "cultural exchange," reincarnate in each others' worlds from time to time, the native acting as host for the visiting time-space traveler. Most likely this exchange provided the background for the EXP skit on the *Axis* album.

—Paul Caruso

EXP

ANNOUNCER:

GOOD EVENING, LADIES AND GENTLEMEN,
WELCOME TO RADIO STATION EXP.
TONIGHT, WE ARE FEATURING AN INTERVIEW WITH A VERY PECULIAR LOOKING GENTLEMAN,
WHO GOES BY THE NAME OF MR. PAUL CARUSO,
ON THE DODGY SUBJECT OF ARE THERE OR ARE THERE NOT FLYING SAUCERS OR. . . UFO'S. PLEASE MR. CARUSO, COULD YOU GIVE US YOUR REGARDED OPINION ON THIS NONSENSE ABOUT SPACESHIPS AND EVEN SPACE PEOPLE.

MR. CARUSO:

THANK YOU,
AS YOU ALL KNOW, YOU JUST CAN'T BELIEVE EVERTHING YOU SEE AND HEAR, CAN YOU? NOW, IF YOU WILL EXCUSE ME, I MUST BE ON MY WAY.

ANNOUNCER:

BU. . . BUT, BUT. . . GASP. . . I, I, DON'T BELIEVE IT.

MR. CARUSO:

PFFFTTT!!!.. . . POP!!!. . . BANG. . . ETC!!?

—JIMI HENDRIX
FROM AXIS: BOLD AS LOVE

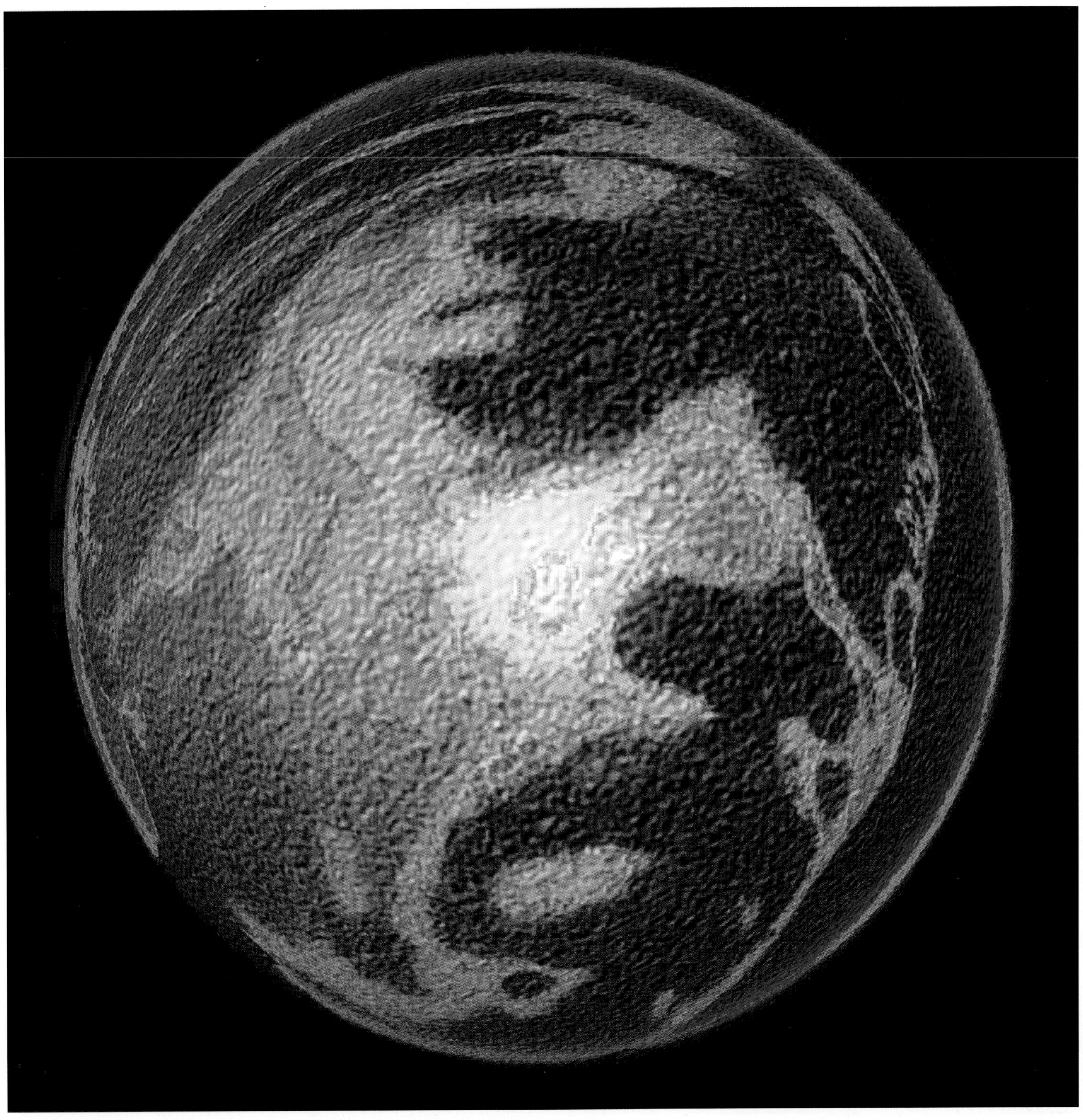

Experimental Photo by Nona Hatay; Colorizing and Imaging by Alice de Young

I was in the Tin Angel restaurant in Greenwich Village, when a friend told me that I was on a Jimi Hendrix album. I had not yet recorded with Jimi so I ran over to the record store next door to investigate this unexplained phenomenon.

It was like having your name skywritten for you by surprise. Needless to say, I was deeply and permanently touched by this unusual person, Jimi Hendrix.

—Paul Caruso

Freedom—a word spoken not only by black people but by a whole generation during the 60's. It is defined in Webster's dictionary as "boldness of conception or execution." Jimi Hendrix's search for personal freedom took this Seattle-born American to distant shores and uncharted musical regions. Few in the music realm waved a higher banner for freedom of creative expression.

—Cornelius Grant

Painted by Nona Hatay; Imaging by Tammy Schatz

Experimental Photo by Nona Hatay; Imaging by Michael "Bongo" Grabscheid

In a world permeated with plasticised feelings, complacency, insincerity and insensitivity, Jimi roared, laughed, screamed and danced his way through an all-too-short life with a naked innocence that will be missed by more than a few.

—John McLaughlin

I'M TRAVELING A SPEED
UNKNOWN TO MAN
AND I CARRY LOVE FOR ALL
IN THE MIRROR OF MY HAND
I SAY LOVE FOR ALL ...
DON'T TRY TO RUN AWAY ...
LOOK AT THE MIRROR OF YOUR HEART
FACE THE TRUTH TODAY —
I AM WHAT I AM THANK GOD
SOME PEOPLE DON'T UNDERSTAND
HELP THEM GOD
I SAY FIND YOURSELF FIRST,
AND THEN YOUR TOOL
I SAY FIND YOURSELF,
DON'T YOU BE NO FOOL ...
YOU ARE WHAT YOU ARE THANK GOD
YOU GONNA SHINE LIKE A STAR
WITH THE HELP OF GOD —
BUT WE MUST FIND OURSELVES FIRST
AND THEN OUR TOOL ...
FIND YOURSELF FIRST
DON'T BE NO FOOL

—JIMI HENDRIX

Songs are like a personal diary. Most of the songs, like *Purple Haze,* were about ten pages long, but we're restricted to a certain time limit so I had to break them all down. Once I'd broken the songs down I didn't know whether they were going to be understood or not. Maybe some of the meanings got lost by breaking them down, which I never do now.

—Jimi Hendrix

Beverly Rodeo Hyatt House
360 North Rodeo Drive
Beverly Hills, California

Angel Came down from Heaven
yesterday --- She stayed with
me just long enough for to rescue me.
And She tells me a story yesterday -
About the ~~[illegible]~~ Love between the moon
and the deep blue sea —
And then She spread her wings
High over me — And She said
'I shall ~~[illegible]~~ read you ~~[illegible]~~ tomorrow'
And I said "fly on my sweet Angel
fly on through the sky — fly on my
Sweet angel ; tomorrow I hope to be by
your side —

And Sure enough this
morning Comes to me — With Silver
wings sillovette against the glow of
the child sonrise -
And my angel She said unto me
"You're ~~[illegible]~~ living through me ..
~~[illegible]~~ still ~~are~~ tears in your eyes -
But why are there

forget about living in the past
My Love and try to realize
I have come, to melt away,
Your pain and sorrow ... forever ."
And I said 'fly on my Sweet angel, fly on through
the sky .. fly on my sweet angel - ~~[illegible]~~ Help me
through the Sky . Help me Come ~~[illegible]~~ alive Take me ~~[illegible]~~ in your life

Colorizing and Imaging by Michael "Bongo" Grabscheid

Above my bed your Angel hangs
Flying on, flying on
Long after I close my eyes
I feel the colored wings
Gently cooling me.
I hear the liquid music still
Coming back to haunt me.
—Robin Sylvester

REMEMBERING JIMI

In my travels, I have been fortunate to meet wonderful people who knew Jimi Hendrix and who have shared their stories and memories with me. Some of his friends have been very generous with their time and have written their personal reminiscences. I feel it is important to give readers a rare glimpse of the real person Jimi was, in contrast to the media image that was given to the public. These stories are very precious to me and I thank people for their willingness to share them for this book. —Nona Hatay

---

In the fall of 1969 I was in New York to cut a rap album entitled *You Can Be Anything This Time Around*. Alan Douglas was the producer. Whenever Jimi and I were in New York at the same time we used to hang out together, talking about cosmic matters. Jimi generously offered to sit in on the recording session and lay down some background tracks. It was a memorable event for me. Jimi playing the bass guitar with his left hand, Steve Stills, John Sebastian, Buddy Miles on drums. Jann Wenner was in the control room grumbling that he wasn't allowed to touch the mixing dials. Anyway, the record sure had a great beat. I was proud as could be to share this moment with the man I believe to best represent the spirit of the 1960s. —Timothy Leary.

I first heard Jimi play in the summer of '66 when we were both performing at the Cafe Wha in Greenwich Village, New York. By the third song of his set the audience was going wild and I was close to tears.

A few days later Jimi came to one of my group's shows and afterwards he came backstage and introduced himself. Unlike what I had seen on stage, off stage he was quiet, polite and very shy. We soon became friends and often went to each other's shows and rehearsals. Sometimes just the two of us would jam together in the basement of the Cafe Wha. What a thrill!

In the Spring of '68 Jimi asked me to play guitar on his song *My Friend* which is on *Cry of Love*, the last complete album he recorded. During a dinner break at that session, Jimi entertained us with hilarious stories about his days as a paratrooper. His huge hands and expressive eyes punctuated every detail.

I mention this because although he was considered the world's greatest guitar player, what I remember the most about Jimi is that he was just fun to be with. He was funny, kind and intelligent. It was a privilege to have known him. —Kenny Pine

---

Although I was less than a year old when my father died, I have heard a great deal about him from my mother. In some ways, I feel very spiritually connected with him, while in other ways, I feel somewhat abandoned by virtue of the fact that I grew up without a father. I find his music to be essentially timeless as evidenced by his popularity years after his death. His lyrics are somewhat of a mystery to me. Although I find his music interesting, I personally tend to be more fond of dance music. Although I have listened to his music at length, I am not really certain as to what his message was. As I approach the age at which he was at the height of his career, given the striking physical resemblance between us, I sometimes wonder what it would be like to have him around as my father. —James Hendrix Sundquist

---

I photographed Jimi Hendrix three different times: on May 11, 1968 at the Fillmore East; on January 28, 1970 at Madison Square Garden, and on June 17, 1970 in his Electric Lady Studio on 8th Street in New York City. As a photographer and picture editor at the Village Voice, where I have now been for 35 years, I had access to movie stars, rock stars, political celebrities, presidents, famous artists, beat writers, and poets.

But Jimi Hendrix was like some kind of God to me, and I was quite terrified in his presence. Here was one of the great icons of the period, the man who played the *Star Spangled Banner* at Woodstock. In those days I was a real groupie, and admired my heroes from the distance of an 80 millimeter lens. Any closer than that I trembled. The times when I was next to him, backstage at Madison Square Garden and later in his Electric Lady Studio, I was afraid to talk to him. I was nervous and scared that I wouldn't get the right shot and was afraid of asking him to pose for a normal portrait.

As I look back on these incidents 27 years later, I am still puzzled by why I was so afraid of Jimi Hendrix. After all, I wasn't afraid of LBJ, MLK, or RFK, all of whom I photographed dozens of times. So what was it about Hendrix? I guess I'll never know. —Fred McDarrah

---

I was playing guitar with the Buddy Miles band from 1970 to 1972. Our band toured with Jimi. Jimi and I jammed occasionally and became friendly. He was a sensitive guy who became overwhelmed by the great fame he created for himself. Because of that he became a victim of his own success.

Being a guitar player as young as I was and at the beginning of my career I had the extraordinary luck of being on the scene while he was making musical history. It goes without saying that the man was a genius and his guitar playing has been copied but never equaled. I myself thought he was the greatest and was horrified at the news of his tragic and unexpected death. I had the honor of playing at his funeral on the same bandstand with Miles Davis, Johnny Winter, Buddy Miles, Noel Redding and others. The whole scene bordered on a circus-like atmosphere but there was also a mood of great respect and deep emotion. I'll never forget it. —Charlie Karp

---

I met Jimi Hendrix in New York City in 1968 through my husband-to-be, guitarist Larry Coryell. Larry and Jimi had a kind of mutual admiration for one another, and the three of us spent many wonderful times together. Larry and Jimi would jam late into the night at the "in" club of that time, The Scene. Sometimes we'd go to Jimi's recording sessions and listen while he made magic with his famous trio. On several occasions, it was just Jimi and I, hanging out. Once he gave me some of his clothes to borrow and I remember feeling some kind of alchemical exchange, a merging of sorts, when I wore them. Jimi always treated me with respect and admiration, and although he made me feel appreciated as a woman, his manner was never coarse or sexist.

Many a wild night was spent with the three of us hanging

out until the wee small hours, listening to Lenny Bruce (a favorite of Jimi's) in Jimi's hotel room at the Drake. Then we'd ride around in his limo looking for all-night places to get some food, then return back to the room where we'd embark upon lengthy explorations of life, the universe, the cosmos, and, always—music.

Whenever I hear one of my sons, Murali and Julian playing a Hendrix composition, it reminds me of those incredible moments I shared with Jimi, who was truly an original. I have met many famous and celebrated musicians in my life, and have even written a book on musicians, *Jazz-Rock Fusion: The People, The Music* (Delta Books, 1976). But there have been very few who have affected me as much as Jimi—not only because of his prodigious talent, but because he was such a free spirit with so much energy, love and passion for life and for people. It was so contagious that even now, so many years later, I can still remember him vividly.

—Julie Coryell

I must admit I've never, in my entire life, met anybody who reminded me even a little of Jimi Hendrix. There was something extraordinary about that guy. He just didn't fit any profiles—none. Although he was not without influences, he remained entirely himself, and didn't model himself on anybody. Hendrix was one of the most alive, aware musicians of his time. He's still making an impression on people who weren't even born when he died.

He took a keen interest in people, people from anywhere. He wasn't concerned with their social status and he was really free about choosing who to spend his time or ideas with. No mistake, though—he was not an easy target. Jimi was smart and very streetwise.

Hendrix was such a complete individual that he was able to get away with pretty fantastic clothes. But his outrageous taste in clothes never suggested for a minute that he might be gay, or soft or unsure of his masculinity. He was what he wanted to be. Jimi was the guy who could borrow my clothes and wear them like they were his. He borrowed clothes from all the women. He loved women. We loved him. It was easy to enjoy Jimi as a friend, in a way that wasn't possible with most male musicians of the 60s. He was pretty uncompetitive and didn't need to worry about attracting women, so he was really relaxed in his relationships with women, women friends as well as lovers.

What Jimi enjoyed most was having a good conversation. He was fascinated by other people's ideas and loved to talk about philosophy and ecology and healing. He was also interested in anything to do with the occult and space. This guy was endlessly interesting, but was one of the best listeners I ever knew. And he loved stories. If you had good ones and would tell them, he'd listen all night. He was curious about how other people lived and their perspectives and philosophies of life.

Most of his original lyrics seemed inspired by people and situations in his life. The most explicit is *Dolly Dagger*, which was written about Devon Wilson. You had to know her to appreciate the song. It was her true-to-life story, all right.

My favorite Jimi story is this: late one night a few of us were hanging out at Jimi's New York apartment after having been up for a loooong time. The phone rang, and Jimi went into the bedroom to answer it. He came back a minute later flustered and excited.

"It's Miles, what do I tell him?"

"About what?" I asked him.

"He said he wanted me to hear something, to get a pencil and write it down." Jimi was upset and a little embarrassed. "How do I tell him I can't write?"

I laughed and told him, "Miles won't give a shit, tell him you can't write and to hum a few bars!"

We all cracked up, including Jimi. It's a poignant story for me because later, when Jimi died, there had been a lot of discussion going on about him recording an album with Miles. What a loss.

I'm always amazed when I meet people to discover the depth of Jimi's influence on them. It stands to reason that those of us who knew him and spent time with him were inspired by him. But often the people I meet are just kids, and their interest in him is as strong as if he were still alive.

I can't imagine ever not missing Jimi. Each year at the anniversary of his death, I am reminded of what a wonderful, funny, sensitive friend and fantastic human being he was. I have never heard anyone say they didn't like him. It just wasn't possible to know him and not to love him. This guy was the future. —Jenni Dean

---

Jimi was a very spiritual being. He knew that the soul and the spirit were eternal. He was aware that we are only allotted so much time to commit to and complete what we are here to accomplish.

There were many sides to his personality. There was the quiet man at repose. There was the excited man-child discovering new complexities about himself, learning that the essence of something is really its simplest form made concrete. He used his guitar to speak a language that everyone now is beginning to understand. His guitar was his lady; his voice and his guitar were one. He tried to communicate to outer space—to inner space, to angels, to people, to spirits, to God as we know Him.

Jimi was my brother. We chose each other. We talked of many things, we loved and we trusted each other. He was to return to complete the *Cry of Love* album but he didn't make it back. And that is where I still am at times. Still waiting, praying, and still loving.

I hope the children who have come after us are catching up,catching on and being true to themselves and their own beliefs. James Hendrix the man lives on in his music forevermore. —Emmaretta Gloria Marks

THANK YOU GOD FOR MAKING ME STRONG AND
THANK YOU GOD FOR STAYING WHERE YOU BELONG—INSIDE ME

—Jimi Hendrix

JIMI HENDRIX—THE SPIRIT LIVES ON...

Jimi Hendrix is now widely recognized as one of the most important musician/composers of our time. Some people thinkof him as a shaman, preacher, magician and he called himself a Voodoo Child. While his work and life clearly stand as their own testament, Hendrix's spirit and message have been kept alive by the devotion of countless individuals. In creating this book, I wrote to people—some who knew Hendrix as a friend, some who played music with him, and others who, in some way, were inspired, enlivened, and healed by his music in order to gain a deeper understanding of the expanded influence of Hendrix.

I received many responses, all fascinating, some quite amazing. These letters brought stories from Jimi's childhood, accounts of the first few times he played out with a borrowed guitar, stories from the Army, stories from San Francisco, New York City and Europe. Some writers crafted fine essays, others beautiful poetry. It was a truly touching outpouring of love.

I was dismayed when the book design and production team reminded me that *Jimi Hendrix: Reflections and Visions* is, after all,was an art book with limited space allocated for text. It was very difficult to decide which comments to include in this book, as all of the writings were equally good in their own way. Ultimately, the decision was an artistic one, in that we had to match words with pictures and consider the entire "flow" of the book.

I had planned to include a chapter called "The Spirit Lives On" which would include stories, tributes and anecdotal material. However, there was just too much material, and the chapter had to be omitted. This was very sad and painful for me, as I knew that people had put time, effort, and a lot of love and feeling into their writings.

I wish to express my gratitude to everyone who wrote something for this book. In the future, their material will be showcased in another format, perhaps in a book or magazine articles. Special thanks go to the following people, whose works could not be included:

—Nona Hatay 1995

Richard Aaron
Marcel Aeby
Brett Alexander
Jerome Preston Bates
Tony Beard
Ellarie Briscan
Reginal "Briz"Brizborn
WesleyBrown
Tony Brown
Alan Butunik
Dave Bynoe
Mario Capitano
Peter Davies
Guy Davis
Ilan Elmatad
Mike Fairchild
Caesar Gleebeek
EJ Gold
Dan Greene
Michael Gregory
Joe Griffith
Jess Hansen
Reuben Jackson
Remy Kabaka
Jacaeber Kastor
Jeff Kind
David Kramer
Daniel Masler
John McDermott
Chris Murphy
Gale Myers
Peter Newland
Dave Pearcy
Vic Peters
Ben Potter
Angel Reca
Steve Roby
Paul Sensan
Michael Slattelka
Don Snyder
Kevin Stein
Jonna Taylor
Tony Vacca
Narada Michael Walden
Charles Watts
Charles Wright

CONTRIBUTORS

CARLOS W. ANDERSON is a singer, writer, and artist and the minister at Hope Community Church in Amherst, Massachusetts. His recent book is entitled *The Gift is Life*.

JIMY BLEU is a New York City musician and actor. He stars in the film *Voodoo Child*.

LARRY BLUMENSTEIN is a New York City artist and collector.

JOEL BRATTIN, Professor of English at Worcester Polytechnic Institute in central Massachusetts, is a writer for *Univibes* magazine.

ROSA LEE BROOKS, AKA Golden Rose, is a musician from Los Angeles. Hendrix co-write and played on her recording *My Diary* in 1964. Her latest release, with Zula, is entitled *Straight on the Rhythm*.

JAMES BROWN, "The Godfather of Soul," is a singer, composer, and recording artist from Georgia. He has sold millions of records.

SEAN CINEMAIE, Hendrix art collector, resides in New York City.

ARI FREEMAN COHEN, formerly a professor of African American Studies at the University of Massachusetts, is a musician and writer living in California.

IRA COHEN, president of Akashic Records, a non-profit organization devoted to preserving the hidden meaning of the hidden meaning, is a poet, photographer, and a member of New York City's Electronic Multimedia Shamanism Gang. His spoken poetry was recently featured alongside the music of Ornett Coleman and Don Cherry on the Sub Rosa CD *Majoon Traveler*.

JULIE CORYELL, writer of *Jazz-Rock Fusion: The People, The Music* (Delta 1976), is a photographer, film artist, and musician living in New York.

BILLY COX, a musician from Nashville, Tennessee, played bass in Hendrix's Band of Gypsys. He was recently featured on the Warner Brothers' CD *Stone Free: A Tribute to Jimi Hendrix*, produced by John McDermott.

MICHAEL CARUSO is a musician and appreciator of music from New Jersey.

PAUL CARUSO was a musician in Greenwich Village in the 60s and 70s, playing with the likes of Richie Havens, Tim Hardin, and Danny Kalb. He currently plays in a blues band and practices alternative medicine.

MONIKA DANNEMANN is a painter living in England. A book of her artwork, *The Inner World of Jimi Hendrix*, is published by Bloomsbury Publishers in England.

BETTY DAVIS wrote and performed *F.U.N.K.*, a song dedicated to Hendrix, on her 1975 LP *Nasty Girl*.

JENNI DEAN, "Queen of the Scene" in New York City in the 1960s, is now retired. She became a mother of four who practices astrology in England.

JOHN DUBBERSTEIN, physician and musician, plays guitar in the New York City band Seizure Salad and sitar on Michael Filgate's album *Ode to Mother Nature*. He works internationally with the World Health Organization.

DU KANE, with Luke Baldry, record on Continuum Records as the group Beautiful People. Their CD, *If 60s were 90s*, layers Hendrix guitar and vocal samples with their own original music.

MAX DRAKE is a poet, writer, and musician from California.

JIM FAHEY is a musician, writer (*Relix* Magazine) and radio producer from New York City.

SHERRY GOODMAN is a historian and professor of modern art. She is presently Curator for Education at the Pacific Film Archives and the University Art Museum at the University of California at Berkeley.

MICHAEL "BONGO" GRABSCHEID is an artist and computer programmer living in Western Massachusetts.

CORNELIUS GRANT is a producer, writer, and musician from Los Angeles.

JAMES AL HENDRIX, Jimi Hendrix's father, resides in Seattle, Washington.

JAMES HENDRIX JR., formerly James Sundquist, was declared Hendrix's sons by the Swedish courts in 1975.

CHARLIE KARP, singer, songwriter, and guitarist, has recorded three solo albums on major labels and performed with Buddy Miles, Aerosmith, and David Johansen. His songs have been covered by many artists, including Joan Jett and Leslie West.

TIMOTHY LEARY, writer and poet, produced a rap album with the Last Poets in 1970. Hendrix played on the album, entitled *You Can Be Anything This Time Around*.

TAJ MAHAL is a composer and musician who has recorded many albums. He currently makes his home in Hawaii.

EMMARETTA GLORIA MARKS is a Woodstock, New York musician who was a back-up singer for Hendrix on the *Cry of Love* album.

YAZID MANOU is a concert and event producer from Paris, France.

FRED MCDARRAH, New York City, has been with the Village Voice since the 60s, where he is a photographer and picture editor.

JOHN MCLAUGHLIN, musician and composer, has recorded albums with many musicians.

MITCH MITCHELL, musician and recording artist, was the drummer for the Jimi Hendrix Experience. His book, *Inside the Experience,* written with John Platt, was issued in 1990 by St. Martin's Press and the Octopus Publishing Company.

FELIX PAPPALARDI produced the group Cream and was a member of Mountain. He died in 1983.

LENEE JEAN PIERRE, AKA LADY SUPREME, is an entertainer, actress, and model from New York City.

KENNY PINE is a musician, composer, recording artist from New York City who played on Hendrix's recording of *My Friend.*

NOEL REDDING, musician and composer, played bass guitar with The Jimi Hendrix Experience. His book *The Experience* was published in 1990 in England.

VERNON REID, founder of the Black Rock Coalition and musician and recording artist with the band Living Colour, is a featured performer on the Hendrix tribute CD *Stone Free.*

ZENO ROTH is a writer, musician, and composer. His latest CD is entitled *Zenology.*

LARS SKANBERG is a Hendrix art collector who lives in Sweden.

EMIKAN SUDAN is a photographer and video artist from Northampton, Massachusetts.

ROBIN SYLVESTER, musician, composer, and recording artist, resides in San Francisco.

BEN VALKHOFF, artist and Hendrix researcher since 1967, is known for his Jimi Hendrix Photo Archive in Holland and for his contributions to various publications.

NORMAN WEISBERG is a writer and publisher from Long Island, New York.

JOHNNY WINTER, guitar legend, was born in Texas. He has issued many recordings from the 60s to the present, including some with the great Muddy Waters.

J I M I: Jimi Hendrix Information Management Institute
Editor: Ken Voss
Box 20361
Indianapolis, IN 46220
(317) 257-JIMI

STRAIGHT AHEAD: The International Jimi Hendrix Fanzine
Editor: Steve Roby
P.O. Box 965
Novato, CA 94948
Phone/FAX (415) 898-4202

THE JIMI HENDRIX ARCHIVES
Tony Brown
28, Chadwick Square
Seabank
King's Lynn, Norfolk
PE30-2LT England

JIMPRESS: The British Jimi Hendrix collectors magazine
Editor: Steve Rodham
108 Warrington Road, Penketh,
Warrington, Cheshire, WA52JZ England
Phone/FAX (0925) 723541

UNIVIBES: International Jimi Hendrix Magazine
Editor: Caesar Glebbeek
Coppeen, Enniskeane
County Cork
Republic of Ireland

JIMI HENDRIX PHOTO ARCHIVES
Ben Valkhoff
Muiderslotstraat 38
3123 RM Schiedam
Holland

THE JIMI HENDRIX FOUNDATION
Director: Kevin Stein
8450 Melrose Place
Los Angeles, CA 90069
(Official Jimi Hendrix Foundation Website: *Room Full of Mirrors*)

HENDRIX ART AND MUSIC PROJECTS
Coordinator: Nona Hatay
P.O. Box 182
Montague, MA 01351
(413) 367–2116

List of *PhotoArtWorks*

All original photographs taken in black & white by Nona Hatay

page

1 *Self-Portrait, Electric Lady Studio*, 1985, Color Pencils

6 *Concert A17*, 1969

7 *Concert B106*,1969

8 *Fly on, Fly on C34a*, 1989, Wax Crayons and Oils

16 *Concert A40*, 1969

17 *Concert A34*, 1969

18 *Entrance B102*, 1979, Experimental B/W

19 *Concert A50*, 1969

20 *Concert A18*, 1969

21 Voodoo Child II *B24*, 1977, Experimental B/W

22 *In the Light B06*, 1979, Experimental B/W
Voodoo Complex I B27, 1978, Experimental B/W
*Voodoo Complex II B74, 1978,*ExperimentalB/W
Voodoo Complex III B40,1979, Experimental B/W

24 *All Along the Watchtower B104*, 1975, Experimental B/W

25 *Dream of Freedom B78*, 1975, Experimental B/W

27 *Elecricity I B19*, 1979, Experimental B/W

28 *First Haze B103*, 1975, Experimental B/W

30 *Manic Depression B22*, 1976, Experimental B/W

31 *Jimi Hendrix I* B37, 1971, Experimental B/W

33 *Star Spangled Banner B62*, 1975, Experimental B/W

34 *Rock Me Baby A19*, 1976, Solarized B/W

35 *Love or Confusion B76*, 1979, Experimental B/W

36 *The Wind Cries Mary B41*, 1976, Experimental B/W

38 *Astro I B88*, 1977, Experimental B/W

39 *Electricity II B55*, 1979, Experimental B/W

41 *Drifting B101*, 1975, Experimental B/W

42 *Emergence B03*, 1976, Experimental B/W

43 *Self & Jimi B23*, 1978, Experimental B/W

49 *Wild Thing C1h*, 1987, Wax Crayon

50 *Bold as Love C19a*, 1982, Inks

53 *Freedom C18b, 1985*, Oil Paint

54 *Standing in Truth C7a*, 1989, Wax Crayon

56 *Sunshine of my Love C1f*, 1990, Wax Crayon

57 *Message of Love C9a*, 1990, Wax Crayon

59 *May this be Love B07*, 1992, Oil Paint

60 *1993 C39a, 1985*, Toned & Oil Paint

63 *Room Full of Mirrors C20a*, 1987, Oil Paint

65 *If 6 was 9 C17d*, 1982, Inks

66 *Up From the Skies c21a*, 1985, Oil paint

68 *Purple Haze* C4d, 1989, Wax Crayon

69 *Haze I B89*, 1985, Toned

70 *Purple Pleasure A33*, 1985, Toned

71 *Orange Passion C37a*, 1985, Toned Experimental B/W

72 *Maui C2e*, 1989, Wax Crayon

75 *Summer Dream C31a*, 1980, Water Colors

77 *Red Comet C45*, 1985, Toned Experimental B/W

79 *One Rainy Wish C26a*, 1982, Toned Experimental B/W

80 *Moon Turn the Tides C22a*, 1982, Toned with Oil Paint

83 *Reverberence C24a*, 1987, Oil Paint

85 *SunLight B45*, 1985, Toned

86 *Feedback*, 1982, Toned

89 *Tapestry C25a*, 1980, Water Colors

90 *Magic Touch C28a*, 1982, Oil Paints

91 *Magic Fingers A41*, 1985, Toned

92 *Jimi & Betty Davis E01*, 1982, Oil Paint

93 *Electric Lady Studios C29a*, 1987, Oils and Crayons

95 *Power of Love 11a*, 1987, Wax Crayon

96 *Rasta Jimi C27a*, 1987, Wax Crayon

98 *Colors C14a*, 1990, Wax Crayon

99 *Blues C28*, Oil Paints

100 *Wild Thing C1b*, 1990, Wax Crayon

101 *Chico's Mural I B106*, 1991, Experimental B/W

101 *Chico's Mural II B107*, 1991, Experimental B/W & Computer

102 *Invitation NR*, 1993

103 *Venus Vulcano TA*, 1995, Experimental B/W & Computer

104 *I Hear My Train C13a*, 1990, Handpainted, Wax Crayon

105 *Mandala I NR*, 1993, Handpainted & Computer

106 *If 60's was 90's TA*, 1995, Handpainted & Computer

108 *Rays I TA*, 1995, Experimental B/W & Computer

109 *Rays II TA*, 1995, Experimental B/W & Computer

111 *EXP TA*, 1995, Experimental B/W & Computer

112 *Mandala II TA*, 1995, Handpainted & Computer

113 *In from the Storm NR*, 1993, Experimental B/W & Computer

115 *Purple Haze, Jesus Saves 95TA*, 1995, Toned Experimental B/W

117 *Angel NR*, 1993, B/W Concert Photo & Computer

119 *Visions B51*, 1989, Experimental B/W

120 *Astroman X GDC11*, 1990, Wax Crayon

122 *Studio A B53*, 1991, Experimental B/W

128 *Concert A42*, 1969, B/W Concert Photo

CHRONOLOGY AND EXHIBITION HISTORY

1947: Nona Hatay is born in Giffnock, Scotland, on October 17, 1947, the eldest child of a British mother and a Hungarian father. Her mother is a print dealer and an international expert on 19th and 20th century prints, and her father a physicist and inventor.

1949: The family moves to America, settling in the seaside town of Manchester, Massachusetts.

1960–1965: Hatay spends her adolescence traveling throughout Europe with her parents.

1965: Graduates from Holland Park School in London, England passes City & Guild exam in photography.

1967: Apprentices to Bauhaus portrait photographer Berta Himmler in Munich. PHOTO SERIES: *The Abandoned Suite.* LIMITED EDITION VOLUME: *A Day in the Life of a Boy.*

1968: Returns to the United States and is employed as photographic assistant to George Cushing, Newbury Street, Boston. Moves to New York City. LIMITED EDITION VOLUME: *Three Sundays in Washington Square.*

1969–1971: Works as a freelance photographer in New York City for newspapers, magazines, Capezio Fashion, WNET-TV, CBS, RCA, & CIBA advertising. On May 18, Hatay photographs Jimi Hendrix in concert at Madison Square Garden for the New York Review. PHOTO SERIES: *Musicians in Concert.*

1970: PHOTO SERIES: *New York City/Ellis Island.*

1969–1970: Attends the School of Visual Arts, New York City, studying art and photography.

1972: Daughter Heidi Merris is born in Baltimore, MD.

1973–1976: Moves to San Francisco. Owns and operates Studio Hatay, photography gallery and studio. Attends the Academy of Art and City College.

1975: PHOTO SERIES: *San Francisco.* LIMITED EDTION VOLUME: *Views of Jimi's Views of Life,* experimental B&W photos.

1976: PHOTO SERIES: Experimental expanded portraits.

1977: Hatay's father dies. She moves to a farm at Three Rivers, Massachusetts and starts work on an experimental Hendrix series. Exhibits her Hendrix art publicly for the first time in Springfield, MA.

1978: LIMITED EDITION PORTFOLIO: *The Hendrix Portfolio.* EVENT: "The Hendrix Experience," Spider Ballroom, Northampton, MA, introducing *The Hendrix Portfolio.*

1979: Owns and operates Studio Hatay, photography studio and gallery, in Northampton, MA. SLIDE SHOW: *Jimi Hendrix Voodoo Child* at the Flashback Festival, Northampton, MA. PHOTO SERIES: *New England Countryside.*

1980: EXHIBITS: *Jimi Hendrix,* Rock and Roll Convention, New York City. *Experimental Musicians,* Baystate West, Springfield, MA. SLIDE SHOW & LECTURE: *Hendrix & Experimental Photography,* Northfield Mount Hermon School, Northfield, MA.

1981: Hatay moves to California and is hired as the staff photographer for the Rosicrucian Order World Headquarters in San Jose, CA. She produces magazine covers, slide shows, book illustrations, and documentation of artifacts in the Egyptian Museum. EXHIBITS: *Experimental Hendrix,* Jimi Hendrix Electric Church Foundation, San Francisco, CA. Organized "Hendrix Day" tribute held on April 28 at the University of Massachusetts at Amherst.

1982: Photographer for James Brown's California tour and publicity photographer for Tina Turner. EXHIBITS: *Hooker's Ball,* Eros Gallery, San Francisco, CA. *Experimental Tina Turner Photographs,* Ed Mock's Studio, San Francisco. SLIDE SHOW: *Voodoo Child,* Hendrix Convention, Tucson, AZ.

1983: Moves to Montague, Massachusetts. BOOK: *Jimi Hendrix, The Spirit Lives On . . .* published by Last Gasp, San Francisco. EXHIBITS: *Experimental Hendrix,* Floating Foundation of Photography, New York City. *Hendrix,* Rock & Roll Convention, New York City.

1984: EXHIBITS: *Experimental Hendrix,* Hendrix Convention, London, England. *Experimental Hendrix,* Radius Gallery, New York City. PHOTO SERIES: *Inbetween Moments.*

1985: GRANT: Northampton Council for the Arts. PHOTO SERIES: *Abstract PhotoArt.*

1986–1988: Owned and operated Moments in Time Gallery and Zona's Boutique in Northampton, MA.

1986: EXHIBITS: *Experimental Hendrix,* Hendrix Festival, Chicago, IL. *Glossies—A Growing Exhibit,* Thornes Art Gallery, Northampton, MA. *Night & Light,* Northampton Center for Arts. PHOTO SERIES: *Rose Reversals.* GRANT: Montague Council for the Arts.

1987: Hatay begins applying color to her black & white photographs, using watercolor, crayons, material and found objects. EXHIBITS: *Color-Expanded Noho,* International Gallery, Northampton, MA. *Recent Work,* HoHo's Gallery, Holyoke, MA. *First Color Expansions,* Fauve Gallery, Amherst, MA. *Vero Beach Series,* Zone Gallery, Springfield, MA.

1988: Hatay's son Charles Hatay-Gezork is born in Greenfield, MA. EXHIBIT: *Experimental Hendrix,* Psychedelic Solution, New York City. *Christmas Images,* Museum of Art, Los Angeles. *New Views,* Atchison Gallery, Birmingham, AL. Hendrix images used in MTV segment.

1989: VIDEO COVER: *Hendrix/Astro Man* for Rainbow Bridge Video. EXHIBIT: AutoArt, Vintage Car Festival, Limerock, Connecticut. *Experimental Hendrix,* Rock Art & Artifacts Exhibit, Bridgeport Museum. PHOTO SERIES: *Artists in Resonance,* a photo essay of California artist and musician E.J. Gold, consisting of 21 experimental photographs for his book *Pure Gesture.* Photo series exhibited at HoHo's Gallery, Holyoke, MA.

1990: EXHIBIT: *Jimi's Back*, FNAC Gallery, Montparnasse, Paris. *Hendrix* (experimental piece) chosen as New Year's Card by Electric Lady Studios, New York City.

1991: EXHIBITS: *Color Expanded Hendrix*, Rock Circus, Picadilly Circus, London. *Jimi's Back* exhibit tours France. *Hendrix in Studio A* chosen as New Year's Card by Electric Lady Studios, New York City. Hatay makes a career change to health care and the healing arts, becomes a teaching Reiki Master, studies Integrative Acupressure and home health care. She establishes a practice in Montague, MA.

1993: BOOK: *Charlie's ABC*, a children's book featuring hand-painted photos of Hatay's son, is published by Hyperion Books. *Nouveau Retro* series, 11 Hendrix *PhotoArtWorks*, is produced with Michael "Bongo" Grabscheid. EXHIBIT: *Nouveau Retro*, Terra Blues, New York City. Hard Rock Cafe buys the entire series to exhibit world-wide.

1994: PHOTO SERIES: *I am Divine*, experimental photos of children.

1995: EXHIBIT: *Hendrix*, Space Time & Light Gallery, New York City. Hendrix photo *Belly Button Window* chosen as icon for the Hendrix internet website. Hatay experiments with computer imaging, producing new series of TechnoArt.

SELECTED MAGAZINES AND NEWSPAPERS

American Medical Journal, American Girl, Billboard, Goldmine, Melody Maker, Guitar World, Guitar Player, Le Journal, LA Times, London Times, Musician Magazine, Masters of Rock, Rosicrucian Digest, Relix, Village Voice.

PHOTOART PUBLISHED IN HENDRIX BOOKS

Cherokee Mist—The Lost Writings, Bill Nitopi (HarperCollins 1993).

Inside the Experience, Mitchell & Pratt (St Martin's 1993).

Electric Gypsy (back cover), Gleebeek & Shapiro (St Martins 1990).

Jimi Hendrix The Spirit Lives On . . ., Nona Hatay (Last Gasp, San Francisco 1994).

'Scuse Me While I Kiss The Sky, David Henderson (Bantam 1983).

Voodoo Child of the Aquarian Age, David Henderson (Doubleday 1978).

The Inner World of Jimi Hendrix, Monika Danneman (Bloomsbury, London 1995). Two photos used as basis of paintings by Monika Danneman.

PHOTOART PUBLISHED IN OTHER BOOKS

Return of the Goddess, Burleigh Mutan (1995), photograph of Berta Himmler.

Charlie's ABC, Nona Hatay (1984), hand-painted PhotoArt.

Glands, Dr. Buletza (1982), experimental photo illustration.

Underground Restaurant Guide to New York City (1971), experimental photo illustrations.

Collegic Guide to Philadelphia (1969), experimental photo illustrations.

LIMITED EDITION POSTERS & SILKSCREENS

I HEAR MY TRAIN A COMING SERIES (14 x 17"):

1991: Purple & yellow, 100 printed.

1990: Blue & red, 50 printed. Turquoise & purple, 50 printed.

1987: Navy & yellow, 50 printed. Navy & salmon, 50 printed. Navy & turquoise, 50 printed.

1986: *Orange Glow*, (14 x 17 1/2"), 50 printed.

1985: *Purple Haze*, (14 x 17"), 100 printed.

1984: Poster for Hendrix book *The Spirit Lives On . . . : Purple Haze*, B&W, (17 x 23"), 1,000 printed. *Astro Man*, B&W, (17 x 23"), 1,000 printed.

1979: Poster for The Flashback Festival, blue & purple, (17 x 23"), 250 printed.

1977: Exhibit poster for Images Unlimited Gallery, B&W, (17 x 23"), 250 printed, 500 printed in San Francisco.

AFTERWORD BY ZENO ROTH

To this day, I remember my first encounter with Jimi's music. I felt the breath of eternity. I saw images of a different world in shining, vivid colors, deep and three dimensional, touching the soul. And what I heard was certainly different from what I was used to; it spoke to me in a strange and exotic, although never alien language. This was not rock music or pop music or some fashionable psychedelic product. This was music—and all that comes with it—in a true and absolute sense; a medium to transmit human and universal truth, a higher form of communication, producing inspiration and creativity in the listener's mind.

I have no better words for it, but to me Jimi's music was always living, pulsating and breathing. It had that electrifying quality that can be sensed when listening to great composers like Mozart, Chopin or Beethoven, a certain healing power that seems to unite all great artists who love and serve humanity. This very love makes Jimi's music different. It reaches the human heart in an immediate way, reflecting the ways of our soul.

Jimi Hendrix was always in a league of his own. It is true that he was part of the famed "Rock 'n' Roll Circus," but to label him as a member of any particular "scene" would limit our understanding of Jimi's universal nature. In the end he was not simply a musician to the world but an emissary using music to express his message.

In his lyrics and some of his hand-written ideas, Jimi was also of a superior standard, probably only comparable to the great poet Bob Dylan, who was a decisive influence on Jimi. His lyrics, though less clear-cut and structured than Dylan's, show the same truly original and ingenious power of wording and imagery.

Jimi was, and still is, an evolved spirit who never died. He will be living on as long as we are able to respond to his "sound paintings of Heaven and Earth". He will be communicating with us beyond the borders of time and space—speaking to us in the most elemental and true sense, directly addressing and animating our souls' deepest resources.

And again I remember the impressions—and emotions—I had listening to passages where he truly spoke to us with his guitar. Having started to play guitar myself, I just thought: this is not possible. To get something like Jimi's strange and unexpected information out of this instrument is certainly not from this world.

When I listen to Jimi's music today I still feel this touch from beyond. It is unfortunate that Jimi's true nature was so obscured by his public image as a wild and animal entertainer. Only a few people around him encouraged his spiritual side, recognizing it as what it really was—the centerpoint of his work and life. Jimi's faith in a supreme being together with his sense of mission on Earth were the driving forces behind his immense energy and his endless flow of creativity.

His mission has stood the test of time, overcoming all obstacles and all attempts to weaken and discredit it. It is a mission we all should carry on, work and fight for, a mission with a clear, beautiful and important message—the Message of Love.

I am you searching to be free

the story
of life
is quicker
than the wink of an eye
the story of love
is hello and goodbye
until we meet again